A BRIDGE
THAT LEADS TO
GOD

A FORTY-DAY CONVERSATION WITH GOD

Willis Reed

WESTBOW
PRESS
A DIVISION OF THOMAS NELSON

WestBow Press books may be ordered through booksellers or by contacting:

WestBow Press
A Division of Thomas Nelson
1663 Liberty Drive
Bloomington, IN 47403
www.westbowpress.com
1-(866) 928-1240

Because of the dynamic nature of the Internet, any web addresses or links contained in this book may have changed since publication and may no longer be valid. The views expressed in this work are solely those of the author and do not necessarily reflect the views of the publisher, and the publisher hereby disclaims any responsibility for them.

Any people depicted in stock imagery provided by Thinkstock are models, and such images are being used for illustrative purposes only.

Scripture taken from the King James Version.

Certain stock imagery © Thinkstock.

ISBN: 978-1-4497-6321-3 (hc)
ISBN: 978-1-4497-6320-6 (sc)
ISBN: 978-1-4497-6319-0 (e)

Library of Congress Control Number: 2012914704

Printed in the United States of America

WestBow Press rev. date: 08/24/2012

Introduction

I began to write these pages for my children and grandchildren. I wanted them to know my relationship with God. I am hoping that they will take the time to read my thoughts once I am gone. I did not expect to write a book, but God has taken me down another path. I am humbled at the thought of Him speaking to me.

From time to time you will come across the symbol ***, a reminder to pause and reflect on what you have just read. Too often I have found myself hurrying on to the next paragraph and missing the depth of what God wanted me to understand. This is not to be read quickly, this is instead to be chewed slowly. You will find that I have repeated myself at times, but repetition is for our safety. I have tried my best to keep this as it came from God to me.

I sin and yet God calls me a saint. I sin and yet He still desires to fellowship with me. I am amazed at the Grace of God. Amazing Grace is not just a song to me; it has become a way of life. He has drawn me forever with His love, even though the sin nature that battles the spirit at every turn resides strong within me. And even though sin has tempted me with each breath, God has continued to love me. He has never wavered in His love for me. Not once. Even when my flesh gives way to temptation and I fall, He is there to uphold me so that my fall is not complete.

*   *   *

God says that we are one. He has joined me unto Himself. He says that I am a new creation and that all things have been cleansed. God calls me His child and has now drawn me to write. Over a period of forty days I listened to God speak to me while I enjoyed the sunsets of Tierra Verde, Florida.

During those forty days, God taught me how to die with joy and with a confident expectation. He spoke to me of the difference between Law and Grace. He spoke to me of the One World Religion. It's not coming, it's here.

Then I wrote about Him. And as I wrote, I cried, I laughed and I remembered things hidden in the past. As you read, if your emotions are stirred or your mind gives way to a higher thought, if a tear is shed or a laugh arises, then God got through the clay pot. I have enjoyed my time with God and I pray that you enjoy your time in these pages. May you see Him who is invisible.

Day One - The Beginning

I'm sitting at Billy's rooftop bar, on the Island of Tierra Verde, Florida, watching the sunset. Tourists and locals gather here every evening to watch the sun set into the Gulf of Mexico. They applaud when it does, as if they were at a performance of some kind.

Tonight's scene is quite breathtaking. Fish are jumping in the water; the sun is setting slowly, creating a shimmering path on the water. The warmth of the sun falls gently on my skin, like a lover's touch. The water is still, though a slight breeze blows across my face. I am left wondering if that was God passing by. Tears fill the corners of my eyes as I contemplate that it might have been Him visiting me, loving me. Tears begin to roll down my cheeks as I realize that it will be soon. The sun is truly setting in my life. I am nearing sixty years old. Most are afraid to speak about death, so they try to convince me that I am still young. But I know what young is; I was there once. I am no longer young. As a matter of fact, I am dying.

I don't have an imminent disease or a life-threatening illness that I am aware of. I am actually healthy for my age. But death resides in my being. And as I sit here enjoying the beauty of God's creation, I sense that Death is calling to me. So I answer.

Death, I see you everywhere. In the plant shriveled up in my living room. In the neighbor's cat that just passed away. In the man in the mirror who is not as strong or as young as he once was. I have seen you coming for me for some time now. You're not a secret. We all know you're here. We all know that you will come for us some day and most fear you. Most don't want to talk about you, but they know who you are. And yes, we have all felt the pain and sorrow you bring when you arrive on the scene. Yet I have looked into your empty eyes, and while you may be wise and skillful in what you do, you are not as wise and skillful as God.

As we sit here Death, having this conversation, God is here also. You know that. He is everywhere, listening, watching. He tells me another story concerning you. He tells me that the only power you have is over this body. He says you have no power over my soul or my spirit. He says who I am inside of this flesh will not perish. He says you can't keep me in the grave. So I must tell everyone the news. Yes Death, you will come for me. You already are bringing the beginnings of pain in my body. And I know sorrow and loss will accompany you as you appear. But God defeated you. Many times He thwarted your efforts and at His borrowed grave He kicked your ass. His exclamation of victory was seen in both the visible and invisible realms.

While He was behind the stone in the sepulcher for two days, Christ was not asleep—neither was He dead. He was out and about in the invisible realm. First, he presented Himself to our Father as a spotless sacrifice. His pure blood, never touched by sin, emptied from His body. Payment in full. Next, He went into paradise to proclaim freedom to the captives. Those who had died yet could not enter into God's presence until the ransom had been paid. Do not think that He did this in the spirit while His body laid on a stone table. He was alive in His body. And after visiting the invisible part of His kingdom, He came out through the stone. He walked among us again for forty days.

So I await you with joy Death, longing for the day my flesh will be stripped off and I will fly free from its grasp. No more sin nature. So Death, where is your sting and where is your victory?

" . . . to die is gain." (Philippians 1:21)

Day Two

As the sun sets on another wonderful evening, I find myself at Billy's rooftop bar, wanting to speak to Death again. The egrets are everywhere tonight. Pure white. Beautiful. The air is cooler as the breeze blows in from the north. Birds flying overhead in a flock, changing direction, together as one. Makes me think of unity. Makes me think of how Christ has made me one with Him. For we are all children of God by the faith in Christ Jesus.

Where did you come from Death? The answer is beyond me. You must be the result or consequence of something. Is that what you are? The consequence of a man's disobedience? Of a man choosing to believe a lie? The result of sin? Sin entered the world in the garden and death came in by sin. That's it, isn't it? You have been around a long time. Since the beginning. The Scriptures say that you entered the world through sin and that sin and death are passed on to all men. So I have you in me. Not blaming Adam. I most likely would have believed the lie too. But something interesting happened that day in the garden when you arrived. You saw what we call "spiritual death" that day. You had a part in that scene. Adam losing his intimate fellowship with God. I know that despite his spiritual death, Adam was still able to communicate with God, to sense Him, to love Him. But things were different, weren't they? Like looking through a tinted window, Adam straining to see God clearly. Or like trying to hear His voice over a phone in a crowded and loud room. Lousy reception, if you know what I mean. And though it was one man's fault, God, all knowing, already had a plan in place to redeem us. God chose us in Him before the world was even formed, so that we would be holy and without blame before God, in love, through faith alone. The test is the same as Eden. Trust God or trust the other voices. Adam failed, Jesus finished the work.

*　　*　　*

He loved us then, He loves us today, He will always love us. Even with you, Death, hovering in my genetic pool and inhabiting my skin, He still loves me. Does that bother you? I wonder. Adam didn't physically die that day. Though with you now in him, it was just a matter of time. I wonder how Adam felt when he began to age. When he sensed that he wasn't as strong. Probably a little like I do.

Except Adam knew what it was like to be perfect. I have not experienced that yet. God tells me that I will someday know what it's like. And that bothers you also, doesn't it Death. That's what people need to know. That beyond you lies a kingdom of perfection. A kingdom of kindness. A kingdom where death is no more. A kingdom where sorrow and pain are no more.

Does it bother you to know that those who have trusted in His blood for their salvation now have God's spiritual life flowing in them? Are you upset that we now can hear Him more clearly? More precise? And that He tells us about you and how He defeated you?

Oh, it must bother you. It must concern you that some of us no longer fear you. That some of us know what lies ahead. I'm sure you don't like it. But you can't stop it. So while you go on inflicting pain and instilling fear, I'm going to tell people the truth about you Death. I'm going to tell them about the life that exists after you have your way with our bodies. It has turned into a beautiful sunset tonight.

> " . . . and the day of death is better
> than the day of one's birth."
> (Ecclesiastes 7:1)

Day Three

Wow. Tonight's sunset is amazing. People here around me are in awe of its beauty. The colors are unbelievable. A dolphin has decided to entertain us. I have come to realize that He created all of this for His good pleasure. We are designed to be like Him. We can experience the same pleasure that He senses as we look upon the glory of His creation, of which we, the new creation, are His masterpiece.

*   *   *

I see you Death, lurking in the shadows as I listen to God. You are a distraction, yet one God allows. You love shadows, for there is fear in them, but God is the light that dispels shadows. You also know He has power over you and I imagine that knowledge makes you tremble, for there is no hiding place in which you are safe. You heard Christ speak to me, didn't you? You were within ear shot in the shadows. He told me "The wages of sin is death, but the gift of God is eternal life" (Romans 6:23). Must have pissed you off when He said that.

He was telling everyone that you had a bark that was bigger than your bite. He was telling everyone that you are the man behind the curtain, like in the *Wizard of Oz*. The great and powerful Oz that people feared. The wizard of Oz needed people to fear him so that they would never find out the truth, that the great and powerful Oz was a fraud. He made people believe he had power over their souls and spirits, but he had none. And you Death, run the same game on humans today. But I know the truth; you only have power over our frail bodies. The curtain has been pulled back.

Let's go back to when you first performed a physical death. It was brutal. Brother against brother. Cain acting as your agent. I bet you were elated. I wonder if you felt a little sickened by it all. You know, the first kill. Probably not. There are those here on Earth that so enjoyed their first kill. They feel power flowing in their veins. That's probably more like you. You probably were basking in your power to destroy life. What did you think Death, when God told Cain that his brother's blood cried out from the ground? Did you see that coming? Life in the blood? Crying out from the grave? And God hearing it?

* * *

8

I'm sure you were amazed, for you are not all knowing as He is. All you have power over is this old bag of flesh. You can fill it with sickness, disease and weakness. He will give us a new one, better and greater than the first one. It will be like His. Death, you have seen His body, glorified, risen, pure, magnificent. We also will have one like His. I haven't seen it yet but I know.

Just as the creation reveals the glory of God, the glory that awaits us when you, Death, are through with us, is magnificent, pure. We are His greatest work.

So have your way. Work in me until I can no longer see with these eyes. For I have other eyes that see perfectly clear. Work in my joints, with the pain unceasing. Soon I will be able to leap and run like the cheetah. Work in my hearing until it's almost gone. But I will always be able to hear His voice, forever saying my name and telling me He loves me. Work in me until the day I take my last breath here on Earth. Yet I will breathe again. I will breathe the cleanest, purest air. I will breathe Him in and exhale Him out.

I am not afraid of you Death; I am growing fond of you. I hate what you do to those bound in Religion, how you cause them to live in fear. That great deception. So I must speak, I must write. But I grow fond of the thought that when you are through with me, I will be glorified as Christ. The sunset is amazing tonight and so is a future with Christ.

> "And as we have borne the image of the earthly, we shall also bear the image of the heavenly." (1 Corinthians 15:49)

Day Four

The sunset this evening is what some might call dull. No clouds to manifest color. Just the sun, a big ball glaring in a blue sky. But I think it's beautiful. Tonight's sunset reveals power. The power of the sun. Physical life itself is fed by the sun while spiritual life is fed by the Son. Death is nearby as usual. I'm sure he has been watching the power of the Son from the beginning. Death, don't you wish you had that type of power. The power to give and sustain life.

Tonight I would like to speak with you about sorrow. Yes Death, that part of you that touches our inner being. There is something good in sorrow that I'm sure you never saw coming. I'm sure you didn't plan on it being so, but God, whose plan is greater, He knew. He knew that sorrow could and would teach us lessons. We should learn not to be the cause of sorrow to our fellow human beings, but we should be also aware of the wonderful lessons to be learned when sorrow arises around us and in us. I as a parent have been so sorrowful for the way I have spoken to and treated my children at times. I have been sorrowful for the way I've treated and spoken to my wife. I have experienced the sorrow of a breakup and the sorrow of losing a loved one forever on this Earth. But I can look back on those sorrow-filled moments and see growth in my life. Often in places people couldn't see. My mind, my heart, my soul. And I remember all those who went through times of sorrow with me like I remember a sweet fragrance. God is present in the times of sorrow. Comforting, helping, explaining. I'm sure that more sorrow will come in my life. Death has already claimed a sister, two brothers, a mother, a father, grandparents, a few friends and a cousin whom I loved like a brother. I wish I could have protected him, Michael knew such sorrow.

Sorrow cannot be avoided, so we must find God in it. We must search through the pain and see God's face. We must be God's ambassadors, bringing comfort, telling of the joy that comes in the morning. Telling darkness that it can't defeat light. That pain is temporary and will one day be no more. That tears of sorrow will be replaced by shouts of rejoicing. For we know that this Earth had a beginning and will have an end. All of its crime, hatred, insanity, pain, suffering, and even death will be no more. God is coming for us. He is bringing a new day, a new way. He is bringing a world party, a celebration that will never end.

*　　*　　*

One last word, Death, before I retire for the evening. I see you for who you are. A tool. Nothing more, nothing less. An instrument to bring us out of this madness and into joy. We will meet on my so called deathbed. It's truly a resurrection bed, you know that Death, even if most people don't. And Death, when we meet, I will look into your eyes and welcome you. Together we will be used to show again the resurrection power of God.

> "That I may know Him and the
> power of His resurrection . . ."
> (Philippians 3:10)

Day Five

No time to enjoy the sunset, even for a few moments, this evening, Death is here early, waiting for me. We are starting to understand each other. He thinks we are all afraid of him. I was young when we first met, three maybe four. Do you remember Death? I witnessed the pain you could bring before I saw you. My mother was pregnant at that time with Timothy. That is all I would ever know about my brother, his name. Because you Death, came and took him.

I remember the love my mother had for Timothy when he was in the womb. My mother would rub her belly with the kindest strokes. She would let me do it as well while she spoke sweetly about my brother that was arriving soon. My father would sing Dean Martin songs with his head gently resting on my mother's belly. I saw their love for Timothy and for me. When the time came for Timothy to be born, my parents left the house, excited but not hurried. They were quite calm since they had done this a few times before. But I was not ready for what followed. The phone rang and Nanny, my mother's mother, answered it. She became very quiet, tense. As she hung up, she wiped away some tears.

Sadness filled her heart and I could see beyond her attempt to act normal.

I don't remember asking what was wrong, I would not have understood if she had told me. The next morning my parents returned from the hospital. They were in such pain. Not the physical type, but the emotional type. Deep, deep pain, the kind of emotional pain that even affects the body, causing it to ache. I hid under the dining room table. I didn't know what else to do; I had never seen pain like this before. The dining room table had a long tablecloth that hung nearly to the floor, enabling me to not be seen. I cried because I was afraid. I didn't understand what could cause my parents such torment. It was the first time I saw my father cry. It was an anguished cry. I didn't see Timothy die that night; I didn't see you come for him, Death. But I experienced the fear that clings to you like cigarette smoke on clothes and hair. I saw the sorrow that accompanies your arrival.

I was terrified of you at that moment. I am not afraid anymore. I have learned the truth concerning you and have discovered the joy that lies beyond your reach. Another place, another body. A better place, a place where God dwells and where sin is no more.

*   *   *

I no longer fear your inevitable arrival at my doorstep. There may be sorrow, there will be pain most likely, but there will not be fear. For I know that this body will perish, yet who I am in my soul and spirit will live on. The butterfly is God's proof to me. Spring is evidence.

Death, you have no eternal power, no eternal grasp. The day you come for me you will release me from this prison of dirt. Death, you will remove my last connection with the dust and I will be like Christ.

"And I give unto them eternal life;
and they shall never perish . . ."
(John 10:28)

Day Six

nother sunset. Different, as usual, but great, as usual. They come to see it. The bar is full tonight. The clouds are as cotton, slowly moving across the sky. A blue sky. Once again I get to see the majesty of God. It takes place always, everywhere. I get to see the sunset here on my perch and I love it.

Do you remember coming for me Death when I was twenty three or so. I can't remember exactly, but I was close to that age. You almost had me death. Damn, you were so near I could feel your breath on my face.

Shooting heroin with a dirty needle will always bring Death running. And so it was that day. Craig, my close friend, and I shared a love of music, women, and heroin. We also shared a dirty needle. You loved that didn't you Death? Hovering in the corner, praying to your boss that we would do it. And we did. I had a temperature of a hundred and five degrees. I had it for four days. I was hot and delusional. My wife went through it with me although I tried to hide the real reason for my fever since she wasn't aware of my heroin use. She thought I had the flu until I woke one morning with yellow skin and yellow eyes. On the fifth day she rushed me to the hospital and the doctor knew what was taking place simply by looking at my yellow appearance. I hallucinated like never before. I was dying. My internal organs were dehydrated beyond repair. I was losing fluid quicker than they could put it in me. Now that's a fever.

The doctor, I don't really know the man, then or now, comes into the room and asks me where my parents were. Are you crazy? Like I would tell the doctor and hurt my parents even more than I had in my self-filled life. No way. So the doctor told me that I was dying. That the liver and kidneys where just about gone. Dehydration he said. I cursed him out and told him to get the hell away from me. I cried hard. I knew I was dying, I could smell it. I sensed it. So I prayed like never before. I told God that I was a liar. Yes a liar. That every time in the past, when I had asked for His help and told Him that I would do better, I had lied. Not because I wasn't willing. Because I wasn't able. That night, in that hospital in Las Vegas, I told God I like drugs, been doing them for years. Ten years or more at the age of 23. I told the truth. I told Jesus that if He would spare my life, if He would give me one more chance I would give Him everything I am or will be. God knew at that moment that I could not get better. Or be better. He knew that even my promise that day I could not keep. And yet He bestowed His grace upon me. I fell asleep after that prayer and awoke healed. Can't really explain it, even the doctor was dumbfounded. It was my miracle. I truly don't care if you believe in them. I have my own as evidence to me. God spared my life. I saw you Death. I was afraid. But you know now that I have grown in my understanding of things spiritual. I know your game and how it's played. I do. You are the one who will take my flesh away, yet not my life. My life belongs to God. Thank you for your part in that upcoming moment when I will see God face to face. I saw you in that hospital in Las Vegas. I see you now. You look smaller.

*   *   *

" . . . thou art loosed from thine infirmity." (Luke 13:12)

Day Seven

Tonight the sun is hiding behind the clouds. We know it's there, we can see the light. It's looking like rain. Yet it often looks like rain and then it's gone in an hour down here. Weather travels fast here. The possibility of rain produces the thought of being clean. Pure. Rain falling like blood on the sin, washing it away.

*   *   *

Death, do you hear me? Did you feel let down at the virgin birth? Your leader didn't tell you about Jesus, did he? Jesus didn't have sin in Him because of the virgin birth. Therefore you couldn't have Him. That was a revelation for you, wasn't it Death? You thought you had us all. Your fearless leader didn't mention Him. Hell no. Your leader is like someone who thinks he is the toughest dude in town. And everyone else does too. But your leader knows that there is another. Tougher. Much stronger. Wiser. But he doesn't tell anyone. It would diminish his power in the eyes of the people. It would harm his prestige. Christ, the more powerful One, goes unnoticed by most in society. He is meek and kind and gentle and loving. He doesn't fit in this world of dog eat dog. So He goes unnoticed. But He is more powerful than sin, than death and than the leader of the rebellion, Lucifer. Lucifer knows that someday all will know. The angels already know. On both teams. They know who the winner and loser will be.

The only ones who seem not to know are the human beings. We are always a day late and a dollar short. We still don't believe that it is finished, that death has been defeated. And that we, by faith, have been already made new by God.

*   *   *

We must see ourselves from the viewpoint of God. We are sanctified, clean and set apart for Him. We are justified, declared not guilty in the courtroom of heaven. We are glorified, like Him. This is not only a declaration, this is a reality. God has declared it to be for all those who have faith in Christ. Why Christ? It was He who defeated death. He who rose from the grave. The virgin birth bothered you, didn't it Death? You couldn't have Him. You couldn't kill Him. If He chose to live for eternity Death, you couldn't have touched Him. And yet He willingly offered Himself up as a sacrifice. The innocent for the guilty.

*   *   *

Death, you couldn't resist manhandling the One who had no sin in Him and no sin on Him. You loved seeing Jesus in the grave, even though there was no such place designed for Him on Earth. They put Him in someone else's spot. You rejoiced at the chance and you did your best. But He ruined your joy when he rose from the grave.

Wayne Brady, the comedian and singer, has a song called *Ordinary Life*. Now it's a good song, but there is no ordinary in Christ. Everything with Him is extraordinary. I can't say it enough, although repetition is for our safety. So I will again have us think on these words: Bigger, Larger, Greater, Smarter, Wiser. Those words describe Christ. That's Him. No Ethiopian can out run Him. No Andre Bocelli or Mariah Carey can out sing Him. No Jimi Hendrix, no Stevie Ray Vaughn, no Steve Vai, no B.B.King, no Gary Moore, no Joe Bonamassa, no Jeff Beck could out play Him. Individually or collectively. No government, no matter whether a democracy, a republic or a dictatorship, can overrule Him. No pope or robe wearing person can be as clean as He. He is the highest of the high. And yet He goes willingly into the belly of death. He let you have him Death. I bet you relished the day. You, using Rome. Why not, you have a history with them. But you were denied the privilege of keeping Him. You were denied not just at the grave site, but at His birth. No earthly father, no sin passed down. No sin, no death. For we know that the wages of sin is death. Listen to me Death, you were denied. Won't be the last time.

> " . . . to be absent from the body,
> and to be present with the Lord."
> (2 Corinthians 5:8)

Day Eight

The sunset tonight is as beautiful as ever. But while the world enjoys its splendor, I am a little disturbed. Death has shown up earlier than usual. I typically can enjoy the sunset for a few moments before he arrives. But he was here waiting for me tonight. Trying to scare me I suppose.

He wanted to know if I knew about the children in Bethlehem. I think he was bragging. It troubled me. All of the children under the age of two were slaughtered. Death, you were sent out that night on a bloody mission. Your leader, Lucifer, couldn't handle the thought of Jesus coming into the world to save it. So you Death, butchered the children. I can almost hear the mothers' cries from deep in history. Some things are like that, they travel through time. It wasn't even the Romans that killed the children, you used Herod. It's not that Herod feared sharing his crown. Herod knew he had to relinquish the crown. Listen, focus. We, as a people, have slaughtered our own for years on Earth. Earth is a killing field. Wars and rumors of war. The killings won't stop. Death will be filled. Yet death will cease to be.

Death has had its human instruments. Herod, Hitler, Stalin, Bela Kun, Pol Pot, to name a few. Listen to the words man has created to identify the various degrees of death: homicide, suicide, massacre, mass killings of civilians, holocaust, genocide, ethnic cleansing. Death, you are having your way with us it seems. Brother pitted against brother. Battles and wars. You seem to be winning. Yet I have a question for you Death. Where are those children you slaughtered in Bethlehem that day? Where are they? They are with Him in His heavenly realm. You lose again. Just when it seems you are winning, we are shown that you lose. The children of Bethlehem sing His praises. They will sing at your demise as well, a song of joy. The children of Bethlehem are alive and well with Jesus. And the sunset turned out nicely as usual.

> "O death, where is thy sting? O grave, where is thy victory?" (1 Corinthians 15:55)

Day Nine

Another day, another sunset. I never get weary of them. It takes some effort on my part to get to as many as I can, but it is so worth it. Not a cloud in sight tonight. As I watch the sky turn a beautiful orange, dusk throws a new element in the mix. The moon is a crescent sliver of itself and there in the heavens, next to it, is Venus. Bright. Not a star as some presume, but a planet reflecting the light of the sun. What an amazing sight to behold. Beautiful.

Well back to the subject of death. Death, do you get upset with me because I take the time to see God's beauty? Does it worry you that my heart is at peace and my soul is at rest? I think if I was in your shoes it would get me angry. I mean, all that you have done to blemish this planet and still the glory of God shines through to us. All that you have accomplished Death, and still people look towards life after you. Well let's talk about John today. You know whom I speak of Death, the one they call The Baptist. Tell me what you hated about him. Was it his passion? Maybe it was that you knew he didn't fear you. John knew from the beginning that he was to decrease so that Jesus would increase. They were cousins born about six months apart. Think they ever spent any time together? Imagine those conversations, dripping with spiritual life. You probably overheard them didn't you Death? They didn't need to speak in a whisper, they weren't afraid of you. Some people wondered if John was the Christ. Did you Death? You're not all knowing and neither is your leader. Did you wonder if John was the Christ? I mean, your leader doesn't tell you everything. He just uses you. But John would not keep it a secret. His testimony went like this as he saw Jesus approaching to be baptized: "Behold the Lamb of God which takes away the sin of the world" (John 1:29).

* * *

You just had to kill John after that profession, didn't you Death? And the way you did it was once again shameful for humanity. You can always count on us humans to do your bidding, can't you? You chose Herod to do your work, but John was not afraid of him or you. I know with every fiber in me that you hate when we are not afraid. I think that's what you fear. We know you have no lasting claim on us. We know you will perish someday, better yet cease to be. And when we display that faith at the time of your arrival for us, fear fills your eyes. I know that when the executioner was sent to the prison to get the Baptist's head, he was calm, he was ready for you. It wouldn't surprise me if he told the executioner that it was alright. Probably forgave him also.

What a term you have created. Executioner. An instrument of humanity, a puppet with strings attached to you Death. But you couldn't get John to fear you. There are more of us every day that do not fear you. We are growing in number. And we will proclaim your defeat and His victory. We will shout from the mountain tops that Christ has given us eternal life. Though we die on this Earth, yet we shall live again forever in His presence. If I could win you over to His side, I would. For I believe that is His heart. To reach the lowest of the low. Those whom this world has discarded and forgotten. The king yes, but also the beggar, the thief, the murderer, the rapist, the executioner. He wants to reach them all and rescue them from the fear you bring. Death, you will never keep us down. We were created from the dirt, not for the dirt to be our end. We have felt the kiss of God and it is sweet. On our last day here, you will enter the room for us and see that He is there also. So take us from this body of death. Take us from the filth of this world. And watch us fly from the room, hand in hand with the angels, singing the praises of Him whom you can never defeat.

*   *   *

I can't wait to pass through the center of a billowy cloud on my way home. I think about it every time I see one in the sky. That's why we meet here at Billy's, Death. So I can be reminded often of my destiny. I cannot wait to smell the fragrance of heaven. I want to see Him in full glory, love emanating from every pore of His being. We will be like Him, a mirror image. For we were created anew in the image and likeness of God. If that is hard to imagine, then let faith leap the gorge. You know, the Grand Canyon called unbelief.

Faith lets me see the future and even though I can only see through a tinted window, a glass darkened, I know it will be even better than I have dreamed. The sight, the sound, the smell of heaven. Better than here, better than my imagination. I see God in everything, in everyone. In darkness and in light. In sorrow and in joy. But not in you, Death. You are not His. He didn't create you. He uses you. As I said before, you are the consequence of a bad choice. He doesn't claim you as His. He is life. Now allow me for a moment Death to enjoy the last of this sunset. We will meet again tomorrow. I have a question for you about Jairus' daughter.

> "He must increase, but I must decrease." (John 3:30)

Day Ten

The wonder in watching the sunset every evening is the rest that it brings to the soul. The work of the day is over and I can feel the stress slowly leave my mind and body. The soul wants to fly and a smile covers my face. I have colors to contend with instead of problems. I feel the warmth of the sun instead of aches and pains. Yesterday doesn't enter the scene. Tomorrow isn't a thought. Only now matters. Refreshing, energizing, calming. If this moment would last forever it would be as close to heaven as I can get this side of death.

Death, you seem to be always lurking somewhere nearby. I see you. How many do you take in a day? How many people suffer because of you? I would think you would get tired of what you do. But you don't, do you Death? No it seems you get stronger and bolder.

I wish they all knew the truth about you. I wish they all knew that you are not someone to fear. That you are simply the one sent to rescue me from this flesh. It is just a matter of perspective, isn't it Death? I can fear your arrival because of ignorance or I can take the time to be informed about you and your ways. I can choose to see the reality of your coming for me, or I can pretend you are afar off. When in reality you are close. Life is so short here on Earth. We act as if we will always have another day. But you know that's not true, don't you Death? So let's talk again for a little while, shall we, as the sun sets on us all.

Do you remember Jairus? Yes that one. He was one of the rulers of the synagogue at Capernaum. I imagine he was in the synagogue the day Christ healed the man with the withered hand. I am sure he heard about Jesus. Jesus was full into revealing Himself to be Israel's messiah by this time. Death, do you remember? I know you do. You just don't like to talk about it, like humans don't like to talk about you. Jairus came and fell at Jesus' feet. Now that must have been a sight. Jairus' daughter was sick unto death. You were coming for her. He begged Jesus to come quickly and touch her so that she would be healed and live. Jesus said yes, He would go with Jairus to his home. But while they were walking together, a servant came and informed them that the little girl had died. I bet you were puzzled when Jesus told Jairus to not fear, to only believe.

They continued on to the house, which was strange, don't you think Death? It was too late for Jesus to heal her. So what did He have up his sleeve? When they arrived at the house there were many people weeping and wailing in pain.

Jesus asked, why make such a ruckus, she isn't dead only sleeping. I bet you thought Jesus had gone crazy. You knew she was dead. You had taken her. People laughed at Jesus and mocked Him. They knew she was dead.

Well, you know what happened next. All the mourners and musicians were asked to leave and Jesus told Jairus and his wife, Peter, James and John to come with Him to the room where the little girl was lying dead. He took her hand into his—I'm sure it was getting cold—and said to her, little girl arise. She immediately arose and walked to her parents.

Can you imagine their joy? Oh, I forgot for a moment that you were there. You saw it happen. You don't need to imagine. He told you to let her go and you had to obey. You always have to obey Him. You see death, I know and I want everyone to know. You must bow to Him. You have no permanent power over us. For when I will see you coming for me, it will mean Jesus is near. Heaven is preparing a welcome home party. I bet my mother and father, brothers and sisters, cousin and friends who have already dealt with you have been given notice that I will soon arrive. So I ask you, why should I be afraid of that? As I watch the sun set on both this day and my life, I know after you have your way with me, I will hear His voice tell me to arise. That will be sweet, won't it Death? I will hear His voice call my name and welcome me home.

*   *   *

"For what is your life (here on earth)? It is even a vapor, that appears for a little time, and then vanishes away." (James 4:14)

Day Eleven

Tonight's focus is the wind. Cool, strong breeze blowing in from the northwest, heading southeast. But it's not cold, it's refreshing. The wind hits me dead on, full in the face, as I sit here, facing the sun. The wind doesn't distract from the beauty around me. It actually enhances it. I see the trees and they are dancing. The wind is their music. The clouds overhead are scarce. The blue sky, ducks in the water, Gerald Albright playing sax, a song called *Get on the Floor* in my earphone. It's another wonderful night in the presence of God. His majesty keeps in wonder, like a small child. What will it be like there with Him? I wonder all the time.

*   *   *

Well Death, tonight we visit the sight of one of your most incredible defeats. I don't care if you want to participate or not, just listen. You have seen Him in action, healing people that you had in your grasp. Surely you have seen Him. But you can't look Him in the eye, can you? Can you imagine? The Son of God, God Himself in humanity, walking on the earth. Can you imagine His eyes? This sinful man would have trouble making eye contact, but His love will draw me into an eye to eye encounter. I will look at Him and He will look at me and we will be one. I am sorry Death that you will never know this feeling. Never look into His eyes. So Death, what did you think about Him? You had seen Him heal the leper. A person who would have been better off dead. He touched people who had the most infectious disease. He was considered unclean by Israel for doing so. You noticed something other than the miracle, didn't you Death, I did. You noticed His love. His love for everyone. The lowest of the low and the sickest of the sick. From the throne to the manger, He came and reached out to all humanity. He chased me for what seems a lifetime. Death, you remember His love. You two were about to meet again, weren't you? At the tomb of Lazarus. Tell me if I'm wrong. Lazarus was one of the few. He truly believed and knew who Jesus was. He was one of the few that looked into His eyes and saw something that others missed or rejected. Lazarus saw the love without judgment. He was accepted as he was. So were his sisters, Martha and Mary. You knew them too Death. Will you tell how their souls and spirits were pulsating with life when you came for their bodies, as they longed to see Him again? They didn't fear you when you came for them. They knew you couldn't hold their brother and they knew you had to listen to Him who is greater.

Here's the funny thing. Jesus was on His way to Bethany, the home of Lazarus. That's when Martha, the anxious one, met Him along the way and told Him that Lazarus was dying. She begged Him to come quickly. You remember that Death, you were there. Last time I looked, you have been everywhere life has been.

Remember what Jesus did, Death? He stopped and rested on that spot, a mile from Bethany, for two days. He wanted Lazarus to die. He was offering him to you. You must have been elated. But it was not a sacrifice, was it Death? It was proof. Proof that He had power over you. And remember hundreds were following at this time. He had healed, preached and loved sinners for three and a half years. They were following Him hoping to get a touch or a look. The twelve actually had to handle security in a sense.

Now God was going to answer Jesus' prayer at the tomb and reveal His power over death. Jesus was heading to the feast. The Passover. Every Jew would be there if they could. It was a longing in their heart. A love. A Law in the hearts of many. His mother would be there. His brothers and sisters too. They all traveled far. There were hundreds, remember Death? They threw palm leaves and their outer coats on the ground as He arrived at the city gates. They cried out that He was the Messiah. Death we know this battle was not waged in private, not behind closed doors. It was waged in public, so that all would know.

Back to Lazarus. Jesus waits two days and lets you have His very good friend. I bet you had a celebration. Did you get applause from the gallery of the fallen? I am sure you did. Why did He wait Death? We both know Jesus waited so that you could take Lazarus. Jesus could then show the world that you had no power over Him. It was show time. I don't know precisely what you were thinking but I can imagine you were confused. Death, you had heard that He was coming to do battle with sin and death. But I am sure you were hoping He was a fraud like so many before Him. But He was the real deal, wasn't He Death. He knew it, you knew it. Can you imagine the scene with me? Jesus comes into Bethany with hundreds following. The throng growing for months. Martha runs to Him and says, Lord, if you would have been here, my brother would not have died. That's what she said, isn't it Death? Yes, but it's the next line she uttered that gives me chills. "But I know now, whatever you ask of God, God will give it to You" (John 11:22). What a declaration of faith. She knew He had power over you.

Jesus said to her "I am the resurrection and the life, he that believeth in me though he were dead yet shall he live" (John 11:25). Jesus asked the crowd to move away the

37

stone from the entrance of the tomb. Did you understand the religious consequences of that action? No man was considered clean that touched the grave of another. Martha cried out that he has been dead four days, surely he stinks. The crowd following the Christ for months was diverse. There were spies sent by the religious leaders to spy out His liberty. They were either hoping that He would fail at this miracle or succeed and give further evidence as to why one must die instead of many. There were people watching, wanting to believe. They liked His words but needed more proof. There were people who were already convinced He was the Messiah. His disciples leapt at the opportunity for Him to show His power, His love.

His disciples had learned to obey Him not from fear but from love. They were hoping that He would be crowned King of Israel. They moved the stone, then Jesus, with a loud voice, shouted for Lazarus to come forth. The power of God went into the belly of death and brought back a man who had been dead for four days. Death, you swallowed him up but Jesus called for him to come forth. Lazarus came walking out, still partially wrapped in his burial wrappings. No more arguing that Jairus' little girl was only asleep. Four days in the grave this time. The crowd was ecstatic. They praised God in shouts of joy and ran to tell everyone they could that the Messiah was among them. The spies ran off to tell the religious leaders the news. Word of this miracle reached Jerusalem before Jesus reached the city gates. I don't know what Lazarus' sisters felt for sure, but I imagine their faith and love grew immensely for Him. Mary was the one who broke the alabaster box of burial ointment and poured it over His head, and washed His feet with her hair. She wasn't the good sister therefore she found rest in His presence and in His Grace. Martha worked feverishly to prove her love for Him. Religion still had a grasp on her. But that's another story for another time.

Death, you are about to face your greatest defeat. Jerusalem awaits. I imagine that Jesus and the twelve, along with Martha, Mary, and Lazarus, broke bread at dinner time that day and spoke about things to come. Hundreds waiting outside spread out as far as the eye could see. The next day Jesus headed for Jerusalem, His face set, focused. He knew what awaited Him. And He was ready. Well Death, another good evening, the ducks are playing in the water, the sun has said goodnight and so must I. We will talk again tomorrow.

> "Then from that day forth they (the high priests) took counsel together for to put Him to death."
> (John 11:53)

Day Twelve

It's been cold here by Florida standards. Dropped to forty four degrees last night. Warm in the house without heat. It's about sixty one degrees right now as the sun sets on another day. The sun is warm, a good feeling, like sitting in front of a fireplace on a cold evening.

The sunset is going to be gorgeous tonight. Not much of a breeze, just enough to make the trees slow dance, close to one another in rhythm. The sky is blue and clear. Beautiful is not a word worthy of this sight tonight. An osprey, a beautiful large bird, nests in the treetop across the water. He's high in the air even when resting. Looking down. His head is nestled to one side as he watches for food in the water below. In an instant he flies from the nest and before people can even turn their heads his talons are out in full. Racing to the water and scooping his provision, barely touching the water. He then rises to his nest and feasts.

I think of the amazing creation that we are blessed to live in. All of us everywhere. The desert with its mountains in Nevada and Arizona. California, with its oceanfront and plush greenery. Colorado, with it snowcapped mountains, brisk air. New England, with its Fall beauty. The Midwest, with its farmlands spreading across the horizon. And here, Tierra Verde, beautiful with its warmth, water and sunsets.

We are getting to the end, Death. The day you will be no more. I like those words. No More. But I will be with Him evermore. That's a good word. Evermore. You will be no more. I will be evermore. That sounds good. You know how it came about, Death. You watched. Overheard. I was born in sin. My grandfather sinned, my father sinned, I sin, and my children sin. Hell, I have even seen my grandchildren sin. Remember Death? Genetic, passed down. All I have ever done is sin. On my best days I have failed in one way or another. But Death, you saw Him seeking after me. Calling me, over and over again. He showed me miracles. I've seen Him in people, and I've seen His hand in circumstances and situations. He loved me then, while I was running blindly in the dark. He loves me now, as I stumble to the finish line. He will always love me. Nothing your leader conjures up can separate me from Him or Him from me. We are now one. Nothing can separate me from Him. Not death, not my sin, not my past, not my weight, not my age, not my race, nor my lack of religious zeal. Nothing can separate me from Him.

*　　*　　*

Remember the song by the Stones *Sympathy for the Devil*, Death? I'm sure you do. It was on the top of the charts where you're from. The lyrics were outrageous but true. Your boss, your leader, was there with you when the little girl was snatched from you. Lucifer was there when Lazarus came forth from the grave at the command of Jesus. So you both know, though I will die, yet I shall live.

I would like to explore a verse in the Scriptures with you Death, if that's okay. "Precious in the sight of the Lord is the death of His saints" (Psalms 116:15). The psalmist knew something, didn't he Death? He knew of a homecoming at this journeys end. Christ rejoices in the day of our death. Not because we suffer with pain and sorrow, but because we lose the sin nature that impedes our fellowship with Him. He rejoices because we are the prodigals coming home to the father's house. We are His children. That may be a hard pill to swallow Death. We are no longer earthly; we are now heavenly in His sight, through His Grace.

This Earth is not our home. We are just sojourning here for a season. My allegiance is not pledged to any nation here. We have been given a mission that has been so distorted by Religion. Our goal on Earth is to show the world His love. To show everyone. Not just to those who gather on Sunday mornings, but to all people. We, as a people, as a family, have failed miserably. We judge our brothers and sisters instead of love them. We gossip about our brothers and sisters instead of love them. We hurt each other and cause division within the family.

God views us from a heavenly position and that is such comfort to me. From a heavenly position, God sees us as He sees His Son. Holy and without spot or wrinkle. But Religion has clung to the dust and gravitated to the Law. Death, you love that the Law produces only yourself.

That is what He was trying to show Israel at Mount Sinai. Remember, Death? Anyone who touched the mountain of the Law would be given to you. The Law brings you into action. But His Grace gives life. Grace has caused Him to hide me inside of Himself. Chew on that for a moment or two.

Now we are heading in a specific direction, aren't we Death? In our mind's eye we are heading to Jerusalem. To the cross. To the tomb. I have read God's letters to His children. We have over analyzed them and created denominations to our own hurt. Arguing over Greek words as if they are Gods. When the simple message of the Book, is to love one another. We have become so concentrated on doctrine that we can't see the forest from the trees. Solomon warned us that too many books would bring weariness. But we didn't pay heed.

It's God's letters that reveal who you are Death. They tell of your defeat and of your lack of power to keep. The cross was your finest hour. You were handed the Son of God. Yet He was also the Lamb of God that takes away the sin of the world. You couldn't resist, could you Death? No, for He was summoning you to be there. You were an important thespian in His play that day. Did you think, after witnessing all His power, that you might prevail?

Death, I'm going to tell them what you did to Him. Your leader using God's own people to hand Jesus over to the greatest warring power at that time. Think about it, He was scourged. How in the world is that word even in our vocabulary? This conversation with you Death has been quite a journey within the journey.

> "The days of our years are . . . (70); and if by reason of strength they be . . . (80), yet is their strength labor and sorrow; for it is soon cut off, and we fly away." (Psalms 90:10)

Day Thirteen

For a moment I thought I wouldn't see the sunset tonight. Dark clouds have moved in slowly from the southeast. The wind is warm. It's going to be warmer tomorrow. The clouds keep trying to hide the sun from me. Yet even when completely hidden from sight, the reach of the sun goes to the end of the Earth. I wonder how many miles I am looking out into the Gulf? The water is calm half way up the canal where people in boats come for dinner and drinks at Billy's, and to watch the sunset. It's darker than usual at this time though. But I am hoping that the sun wins this battle and shows itself before the evening is through.

Tonight I feel you Death. Yes, working in my body. I ache. I feel you in my bones and I see you in the mirror. Not long now and you will come for me. I'm almost sixty and I never thought I'd make it this far. Seems you take so many when they are young. Just thought I would be one of them.

I have a question for you, if you don't mind. You have no idea how long each of us has, do you Death? The issue of life and death belongs to God, not to you. But soon you will come for me. What will that day be like? You took my father and mother quickly while others suffer for days and even weeks and months. Will I go quick? Or will I suffer for a while? Only God knows and I trust Him.

Your leader enjoys watching families suffer. Don't think I don't know you Death. I know you. The wages of sin is death. That is how God describes you. The wages of sin. When you come for me, I will ask God for a few more days. Not because I long to stay in this world, but because people may pay attention to me then. You see we tend to cling to last words. I will tell them of the inheritance. You don't like the word inheritance do you death. It's not fair, it's really not fair. I was born with sin, passed down through my father and his father before him. Always sinning from then until now. From coming into the world to going out of the world.

I have never been able to master obedience, or submission, or whatever word the legalists like to use. And still He wanted to pay for my sins. I who inherited sin from my father and became skilled at it, I who fought it as well, but always lost again and again.

*   *   *

He wanted to trade places. The prince and the pauper. He would die for me and pay my debt in full. But there's more. He would give me His righteousness, not only on a ledger book in heaven, but in essence, in reality. A wax off, wax on scenario. The whole world understands that if you do well, you get a reward, a treat. We are taught that since childhood. But the concept of being the bad kid, the one always in the principal's office, the one always getting arrested. The kid that parents warn you about. When he gets a reward, an inheritance of equal value with the Son of God, it blows the minds of the most religious. A joint heir with the firstborn among many brethren. It's called God's Grace.

*   *   *

The religious world embraces the word Grace, but they issue a caution with it that ruins its true value. The religious have fought a war against God's Grace since Paul was given the dispensation. Of course you know this Death; you have been there to count the bodies. They warn us that teaching God's Grace will give people a license to sin. I have found that I don't need a license; I do quite well without one. Death did you know that the concept of God's Grace is the only teaching that elevates the glory of God to its right position?

*   *   *

God is not my co-pilot. As if He needs me. It's not me doing any type of work, simply believing. Any mixture of Law into God's Grace, defiles God's Grace, diminishes God's Grace and will be spit out of His mouth. Yet mankind continues to try and mix Law with God's Grace. Religion wants to work with God and for God, instead of allowing God to do the work. Religion desires that we applaud man's effort. We have become masters at hiding, disguising our thoughts from others, putting on a good show in the flesh. Religion has turned us into double minded men, unstable in all our ways.

*   *   *

Can't hide from you though, Death. Every time I sin, whether in deed or in thought, your grip on me gets stronger. The wages of sin is death. Do you realize what you are being sent to do for me Death? Of course you do. I know you understand what you will do *to me*. And I know that by now you have come to realize what you will do *for me*. You are being sent to free me from myself. It's amazing. No matter how deep we hide in Religion, in work or effort, we are not free from self. Some have a greater degree of mastery over the flesh but all have fallen short of the perfection needed to please God. Perfection is the prize of the High Calling.

Perfection is Christ. And He grants that status to us as a gift of His Grace. Holy is the word He uses.

Martin Luther joined a monastery to escape his sinful self. The world contained too much sin. So Martin Luther hid behind walls, surrounded with Pharisees like himself. Sounds like Religion doesn't it? He hated his flesh so much, he could not love God. For Martin Luther thought himself unworthy of God's love. Religion propagates that idea, with a heaping of guilt, on a regular basis. Martin Luther hated his flesh so much that he beat himself with whips. Yet after countless self-imposed beatings for his thoughts alone, he discovered that even the beatings were not enough to rid himself of sin. That sinful self always showed itself again. One day he understood and believed that the Just shall live by faith. And he wrote *Sola Fide*, faith alone. Not work, not effort, not doing your best, even that is unacceptable to God. The Just, those who are justified, those who have been declared not guilty in the courtroom of heaven, have been declared so by faith alone. Declared innocent in the courtroom of heaven. Satan, the accuser of the brethren, the prosecuting attorney, accuses us night and day. But to no avail.

The blood of Christ is the evidence of our innocence. Not only did the judge of judges declare us not guilty, but he bestowed upon us an inheritance. Imagine that. By His

Grace, not by our efforts, work or attempts at obedience. Joint heir with Christ. Sounds good to me.

*   *   *

Are you ready to remember Calvary with me Death? So much was going on that day in heaven and on Earth. There's so much to discuss in detail that I must wait for another sunset. For I see Calvary and I see beyond when one third of the living will die. Time for me go. The sun has won today. It has broken through the dark clouds. It is in full view as it quickly slips into the gulf. The birds are back, flying to their island retreat for the night. All is well with my soul.

> "Now to him that works is the reward not reckoned of grace, but of debt. But to him that works not, but believes on him that justifies the ungodly, his faith is counted for righteousness." (Romans 4:4-5)

Day Fourteen

Tonight was different, special. My wife Airen joined me to watch the sunset. I didn't spend time speaking with Death. But he watched as we fellowshipped around life. The sunset was even more beautiful because she was here with me. I have no explanation of why such peace and rest come over me while I gaze at the beauty of God's making. It's as if the sun sheds love abroad in my heart. It's as if He speaks to me here, more than anywhere else.

Tonight I realized that God has called out to me since I was in the womb. He has called out to me to join Him in fellowship, every day and everywhere, my entire existence. I have seen Him in places and people since my eyes were opened. Hindsight is a wonderful teacher, but only if viewed through God's Grace.

Let's switch gears and leave Death alone for a while. I have some random thoughts to explore. Religion ruins my view of God. It diminishes Him. I have discovered something about myself. I love people. The human race I mean. And that's all He wanted us to do. Some legalist changed the idea of service years ago. I'm not attacking the Word. I know up from down and left from right. God is in the Word, but not like they teach. Book by book, chapter by chapter, verse by verse, category by category. The essence of who He is, is everywhere in the Word. His attribute of love is seen hidden between the pages. Behind the letters you find a person, not a myth, a fable, or a figment of man's imagination. You find a kind and gentle father. A meek teacher. A comforter when needed. A healer when the heart is broken. A lover, all the things humans desire in a spouse. Look at us; we are all looking at the wrong thing. It's not doctrine we fellowship with, we must fellowship with the person of Christ found in those pages. He Himself said "seek and you will find" (Matthew 7:7).

*   *   *

We have all met God's ambassadors. Others who believe. No matter what type of turmoil and anguish we have experienced in a group setting, we have met individuals in our journey who have shown us love. I was hitchhiking when I was 20 years old the first time I met a man who knew the person of the book. I got in a Volkswagen Beetle and this man had bibles all over his car. But what amazes me to this day, as I remember that time, is that he never once talked about the bibles. He spoke of a person he had met in his life. Jesus. We rode for nearly three hours and not once did he try to get me to pray. Not once did he ask me if I wanted a bible. Not once. He told me he was a sinner. That he had tried to stop sinning but he was always falling away. Sometimes for a minute, sometimes for an hour, sometimes for a while. He said he didn't want to sin but just when he thought he had mastered obedience, that anger, that lust, that greed, that desire for power and fame would raise their ugly heads. Those flaws within our human nature. This man told me about his friend. He told me his friend Jesus loves us all just as we are and that he was a sinner that had been saved by God's Grace. Today many believe that if you ignore the flesh with positional doctrine, with positional truth, your experience will be one of victory over sin. There is truth to that, yet I know that we cannot ignore the flesh completely for it somehow gets through when you least expect it. But hold on to positional truth in Him. It is the truth that sets us free.

See why death can be so exciting? Death will come and shed this flesh from our souls and spirits, freeing them from sin. A taking away of the old man to leave only the new man, with I in Him and He in me. So why fear death?

My deepest desire has always been not to sin. I have longed for that in the depths of my soul. Many of us have, if not all. Religions of the world, all of them, medicate us into obedient children striving to serve the Master. And they do it by bringing in the Law and the commandments. This only causes us to sin more.

I have a question. How long will believers gossip before they call it sin? How long will they hate the homosexual? How long will they hate the abortionist? The terrorist? Don't we realize that only love can conquer hate? Don't judge me. I think that what the terrorist does is insanity. But I was told to love my enemies and to do good to those who despitefully use you. So I venture on in the journey asking God to reveal His love even more to me and shed it abroad in my heart. I don't want to be angry, or political, or religious. I don't want to be earthly, caught up in gossip and slander. I want to be heavenly, loving all in spite of all. So I will cling to His Grace while I journey for I am rarely what I want to be. You see, the things I don't want to do, I find myself doing all the time. And the things that I should do, I find myself failing to do.

> "O wretched man that I am! Who shall deliver me from this body of death?" (Romans 7:24)

Day Fifteen

The sunset tonight is outrageous. The sun is glowing like a furnace, but it's not hot. Comfortably warm. I can't look directly into it, but I would like to. It is beginning to touch down on the horizon and it seems as though it is melting into the waters of the Gulf of Mexico. A beautiful pink hue covers the sky. All is well with my soul.

Death, tonight I thought we could ponder on a few words. There are always two viewpoints for me to contemplate, both teaching me tremendous lessons. There is the earthly viewpoint and the heavenly viewpoint. I would do well to consider both in this journey home.

The earthly viewpoint of the crucifixion reveals what man thinks about God. All of man's hatred poured out in one horrific scene. Tell me Death, did the viciousness of humanity that day nauseate even you a little? Were you repulsed by the depth of man's savagery? Man's history is littered with brutality towards one another. The list of atrocities is endless and continues today around the world. But He was not a mere human being, was He death? He was the son of God. God clothed in skin so that He could walk among us. He wished to reveal Himself in an intimate way.

What better way of doing it than by becoming a man and interacting with us in a way never before fathomed.

From a human viewpoint it was a ghastly scene. One of His own friends sold Him out for thirty pieces of silver. The temple guards came for Him at night while He prayed. The beating began immediately. They mocked and spat and punched Him repeatedly. They knew this would end with His death.

They brought Him before the religious leaders of the day. The ones who people thought knew God. There was a trial, but it was more of a mockery. They accused Him of blasphemy, a crime punishable by death. The high priest demanded that Jesus answer the accusation that was leveled against Him. He was shouting at Jesus, are you the son of God? Jesus simply replied, I am.

There was a problem though; the Jewish people were an occupied people. Rome had invaded the land and taken control of the area. People feared Rome. And while the Jewish court could render a guilty verdict, it could not execute judgment. Rome didn't allow that luxury. So the religious rulers took Jesus to the governmental leader, Pontius Pilate.

I imagine Death that many were waiting for Jesus to unleash His strength and put down the religious and the political powers on Earth. But He uttered very few words, and none in anger.

He was a different kind of prisoner. A lamb going to the slaughter. The beating Rome gave Him was beyond description. Rome, seasoned in barbaric ways, had the man born in a manger in their hands. And they knew what to do. They could tear the flesh off the bone without hitting an internal organ. Can you imagine the practice and the number of beatings it would take to become that skillful? Thirty nine lashes with a cat-o-nine tail. A whip with nine extensions, all with bone attached to the ends of each tail. Those extensions hit His flesh three hundred and fifty-one times. If only that was the extent of His so called punishment. But they decided to mock Him a little by ramming a crown of thorns onto His head. I cannot even imagine the agony. You were there Death; did you enjoy this display of humanity? Then they crucified Him, nailed Him to a wooden cross where He would eventually die. The foot rest on the cross was so that He would not die quickly from asphyxiation but instead suffer for a while. When I think of that day and what mankind did to the God who loved them, I am at a loss for words.

*   *   *

There is no defending the human race. We still kill thousands every day in every imaginable way. We fight wars over resources and power. We rape, molest and murder. Our governments are all corrupt. Our religion is a white washed tomb, clean on the outside but filled with dead men's bones.

On that day, on that hill, mankind showed the world what it thought of God. But Death, listen to me carefully now. On that hill, on that day, God showed the world what He thought of humanity. He poured out His love.

*   *   *

The second viewpoint. The higher viewpoint. God's viewpoint. This seems a little hard to fathom in my mind, but when He turned Himself over to humanity, it pleased the Father to crush the Son. Even in writing it, I do not have full understanding. But I know it's true.

What was God doing on that day, on that hill? Now it's time for me to speak to you Death about those few words I spoke of earlier at the beginning of today's conversation. The first is justification. A courtroom verdict from the highest court and the supreme judge of all. Let me explain.

The evidence against all of us is sin. Every human being born of an earthly father is guilty of sin. And the accuser of the brethren, Satan, stands before God, the judge, night and day informing Him of what we have done. And in my case, there is plenty to accuse me of. The accuser does not need to lie, for I have given him ample evidence against me, as we all have. But we have an advocate, a defense attorney in our corner called The Lamb of God. He does not defend us by trying to say the evidence against us is false, for it isn't. He does not enter our goodness into evidence, for there are none good. Not one.

Instead He introduces to the court a higher truth. Greater evidence to be examined fully in the light. That evidence is the blood that He shed on that day, on that hill. His own blood. Blood that He shed on our behalf to pay the penalty for our sins.

$$* \quad * \quad *$$

You understand how this works Death? Did your leader, Satan, tell you this was going to happen? I doubt it since one of his nicknames is the Deceiver. You see when man failed in the garden, sin and death, yes, you Death, entered into man's bloodstream. And every time a father planted seed into a mother's womb, sin and death went with it. The proof of that is in the news, the papers, the internet, our children. And in the mirror. But Jesus was different, wasn't He Death?

He had no earthly father. He was conceived by a miracle, too high above human understanding to grasp. I know there are those who think that by exegesis or isagogics they could prove this to the world, but it's not by science of any kind that this is revealed to us as truth. It is by faith. And therefore He had no sin in Him and His blood was pure, undefiled. That it what He offered to pay for the sins of the world. And the judge accepted the blood into evidence and gave us a not guilty verdict.

*   *   *

Doesn't it blow your mind that He still loves us when He has watched us for so long and knows us so well? His evidence was His work on that hill, on that day. You could not kill Him Death, for you had nothing in Him or no sin against Him. His blood was free of sin and the wages of sin is death, remember? Think about that for a moment. He could have lived eternally in the earthen body. Death could not have claimed Him. Yet He sacrificed His innocent self for my sinful soul.

*　　*　　*

Justification means that we are just and righteous in the sight of heaven's courtroom. The ledger of sin against us is erased without a trace left. It's as if we never sinned. The great exchange it has been called. He took our sins upon Himself and gave us His right, standing before God. When God, the judge, sees the blood entered in as evidence and the cleansing power of that blood to wash away sin, He rules in favor of humanity. I can't imagine the pain, the agony, but not once did He beg Rome for mercy. Not once did He say that He was innocent. This is why He came to Earth. To justify mankind. Believe it, for faith is the door by which we enter in.

*　　*　　*

"In the beginning was the Word, and the Word was with God, and the Word was God. And the Word was made flesh, and dwelt among us, and we beheld his glory, the glory . . . (of a uniquely born son) of the Father, full of grace and truth." (John 1:1-14)

Day Sixteen

When I first arrived tonight it was getting cloudy. Perfect in temperature, cool yet warm enough to be without sweater or coat. I don't know how to describe it other than perfect. I thought the sunset was going to be less than I expected. The sky was clear just where the sun melts into the horizon. The rays of the sun were slipping through the clouds. Like an overhead searchlight looking for the lost. The Osprey came to see the sunset again. In that, we are one. I wonder what he thinks of me. Every night he returns here, sitting high atop the tree.

It is feeding time for the smaller birds but not for the Osprey. He comes to watch. Does he understand me? He hears me, he sees me, but does he know I love seeing his majestic appearance? He has learned about mankind. We have caged his mother and father and brothers and sisters. We have taken him from the treetops and placed him in a zoo. Yet the caged ones are not like this one. This one is free. He is a king among birds in this area. No other bird can fight him or chase him away. He does not fear many birds. The smaller birds, even the fishing birds must battle for a prime fishing location. But not the Osprey. I have seen him move, he glides across the sky. I have seen him, talons extended, attacking a prey. The Osprey is gifted with speed and power. His beauty is in who he is. He should never be in a cage. Nor should we. Caging only stirs the rage within.

How did we ever get to the point where we would sell human beings to each other as slaves? Not just Africans but slaves of all nations and races. Slavery has been around since the first dawn broke. Child molestation, are you kidding me? Has the human race fallen so far, so low, that some parents turn a blind eye to this type of wickedness? Murder by individuals, by governments, by nations or organizations. Religious motives and political agendas. Love of money.

I need to think worldwide when I think of family. The human race. All of us. Like the colors of the rainbow or a bouquet of wild flowers. You are my brother, my sister, and I am yours. Our governments wage wars against you, not me. I wage war on no one. I fight not against flesh and blood, but against principalities and powers in the air. The invisible which becomes visible at the point of death. Yet the human race has been barbaric since Cain killed Abel. Religion will not stop this barbarism from happening. Religion is the cause of it. Men getting worse and worse. The Law imbedded in the hearts of men.

Lord, slow me down. Let me enter into rest. Let me enter into communion with You. Teach me to not love money. I need to live in your presence and not hide behind a bush. I desire face to face fellowship. I want to hear your still small voice. The world is anxious about many things. I am not of this world, for my home is in the heavens. That is where I am seated above. The world loves war, You are our peace. Lord, come quickly.

*   *   *

"Love not the world, neither the
things that are in the world . . .
(1John 2:15)

Day Seventeen

There is an abandoned dock that can be seen from my perch. I call it *imagination*. I can envision many scenarios. I can go anywhere from this dock. I can sail out into the deep seas or enter into the brush for a journey. To dream is to see beyond what is visible. To go to places where no one has gone before. All new, all fresh. To have a confident expectation that your hopes will come true. This is the dock of adventure and wonder. The dock of potential and possibilities. It awaits our arrival and blesses our departures. It is home. It is a safe haven in a storm, nestled away in a cove. A place to think and plan for the future. It is a choice to nowhere or to somewhere. Enjoy your journey my friends.

Being alone in contemplation can involve music. I believe it should. God likes music. When I write my thoughts on paper, music fills my ears and my soul. Contemplation means the elimination of human distractions so that we can hear ourselves think and so that we can listen for the direction of the spirit. Music helps my contemplation. Both the instruments, with their passion and the vocals, with lyrics that stir our emotions, taking us to a different place. Music has helped me commune with God and it has helped me mourn. It has brought tears to my eyes and comfort to my soul. It has been used by God to bring about my change, my growth. I am a music lover.

Nehemiah was the cup bearer of Artaxerxes, the king of Persia. It was not a good position for a slave for he drank from the king's cup to see if it was poisoned. Nehemiah was not allowed to speak in the king's presence or even make eye contact. He was a slave, a servant without pay.

Yet Nehemiah enjoyed what he did. He thanked God for the position and went to work every day with a cheerful countenance. Love was his countenance and it showed on his face and in his body language. One day Nehemiah brings the king's cup, but something is different. His countenance had changed. He was sad for the first time in the king's presence. Artaxerxes, always paying close attention to Nehemiah, for his life depended on it, noticed something was wrong. So he called out to Nehemiah and asked: why is your countenance sad, seeing you are not sick? If this is something else then sorrow on your face, then I must fear. Nehemiah went on to tell the king about his destroyed city and scattered people. The point is this today, Nehemiah never said a word to the king before this, yet the display of love and contentment was evident to the king and God touched the king's heart. The king, moved by compassion for Nehemiah and his people, promised to rebuild Jerusalem and allow Nehemiah's people to go home. Don't tell me God cannot use silence. He has used a quiet demonstration of love many times.

*   *   *

" . . . a time to keep silence, and a time to speak." (Ecclesiastes 3:7)

Day Eighteen

Religions of all sorts seems so defiled and ungodly to me. I have been impacted by Christianity for nearly sixty years and am best equipped to talk about it. Christianity was designed by God to be a light, a comfort, a forgiveness. It has become an institution of judging and marking. It has become a place where greed and power has gotten a stronghold on the pulpit. Men who know nothing as they ought, trampling underfoot the ch0ildren of God. Israel did it and we are doing it. All religions are doing it. They present fear instead of love. And guilt instead of faith.

The churches of our own creation have abused every passage of the Word. They have twisted the Scriptures to their own destruction. The divisions debate Jesus as if they know. And they use verses from the Book to drive points home, like daggers in the hearts of the doubting. It is a doctrinal war and the casualties are numerous. The wounded are our brothers and sisters. We mark them and avoid them, calling them enemies. We have left a long time ago our first love, Jesus.

When we represent Him, we are not to be as the Lion of Judah coming to conquer those who disagree with us. We are to be like the Lamb of God that takes away the sin of the world. The Lamb who loves us, forgives us, and bestows mercy on us. The Lamb that was butchered in our place. And He now pours God's Grace out of every wound, for there is no blood left in His body. It is on the mercy seat.

*　　*　　*

The churches have the disposition of a lion, hunting. The world feels like game. We need to stop hunting and start loving. Stop trying to win a doctrinal debate and let ourselves be lost in Him so that He can teach us to love and forgive and share. To be like the Lamb is the prize and the goal. To have His kindness and patience. He loved the lepers, the untouchable ones. He touched them with His gentle caring hands. The prostitutes who were publically loathed by the religious people they serviced in the dark. He loved them openly. No fear of contamination or judging in His heart. He didn't care what the people said, He knew the truth. He ate with a tax collector whom the people were taught was unclean, in the unclean man's home. That action was so unclean to the religious of His day, left, right, and moderate.

When I judge another person or mock them, it reveals that self-righteousness still has a grasp on my soul. My nature permits the judging and the church has taught me how to do it well and with passion. I am the most blessed man to live in this dispensation of God's Grace. My heart is deceitfully wicked and desperately sick. My mind has been defiled by doctrines about clothing and music and whether or not I can dance. We judge hairstyles and tattoos. We judge dress on Sunday mornings and Saturday nights. We debate whether or not we can drink wine.

Christianity has failed to show the world the Lamb of God. The church has failed to show the world love. Love is disappearing more and more with each passing moment. Not His love for us, but our love for one another. John had it right, I must decrease and He must increase. Is it too late to make Him the focus of my attention? Not the local assembly, or the pastor teacher, or the doctrine, or the choir, or the tithe, but Him. We need less Greek words and more love. There is no one like Him. Never has been, never will be.

As He hung on the cross dying, He said "Father forgive them" (Luke 23:34). Are you kidding me? What would I have said? He never defended Himself against the trumped up charge. They had nothing on Him and everyone knew He was innocent. Even Pilate said that surely this man is innocent. And the Centurion who was in charge of the crucifixion said that surely this man is the son of God. Am I innocent? Not in the least, guilty as charged. Yet the innocent man has exchanged places with the guilty man and delivered the guilty from debt.

*   *   *

The church was to be the conveyor of God's Grace to a dying world, but instead it is the teacher of the Law. It was to reveal unity to the world, but instead has shown forth division from the beginning. This in no way has diminished who Christ is; it just hides the revelation under a basket.

> "You are the light of the world . . ." (Matthew 5:14)

Day Nineteen

The wind is furious tonight. Blowing in from the south, getting ready to clash with a cold northern front that is moving southward. The warm air wins most of the battles here. It will tonight. It is strong. The sun also is warm this evening.

Warmth, now that is quite a subject in itself. Both in the weather and in the nature of mankind. Having a warm disposition towards people will hold back the cold comments and actions directed your way. Just as the strong southern wind moving north will hold back the cold breeze moving south tonight.

Mankind can be cold at times. And often the coldest comments thrown at us feel like stones. Even ones thrown at us in humor can break the glass windows of the heart. I may not show my pain, but the coldness of humanity chills me to the core.

I have thrown stones and comments at other people. I am not innocent. I fall short at every turn it seems. I have not been the husband I should have been, or the father I desire to be. I have failed friends and God more times than

I can count. I thank God tonight that He no longer marks iniquity nor holds my actions against me. I am forgiven of it all. My heart desires that the same love that He pours into me will be poured out of me. Like water from a shattered vessel.

No matter what title I have worn on this Earth, I have fallen short. Paul the Apostle called himself the chief of sinners. Now that's a title to wear. My prayer this evening, as I converse with God, is that He shows me the depths of His Grace. The height and width of it, the fullness of it. And that I can begin to bestow it upon others. Not just upon those who agree with me or believe with me, but upon all the men and women that I pass on my journey home.

*   *   *

God's Grace produces love. He has bestowed upon me a favor without any expectation of return. Therefore I owe Him nothing. I do not need to work, or study, or pray, or try harder. It is finished. He accomplished all that mankind could not at Calvary. And then He bestowed His Grace upon us freely. God paid my debt, wiping the ledger against me clean. His blood washing the filth of my sin from His view. I owe Him nothing because He said so with love. A firm grasp of the hand, not wanting to hurt me in a show of superiority.

But gentle, kind. Sensing the power He possesses but not afraid of it, in awe of it. Eye to eye, face to face. Not a glance, but a deep look into my soul, heart to heart. Actually an exchange of life. I hope when I meet people, I have the love to look into their eyes and see them beyond the surface, soul to soul.

*   *   *

Grace means unmerited favor. I can't earn it, can't work hard enough or long enough to acquire righteousness. The term righteousness only applies to one, it's another title He possesses. The Righteous One. It doesn't belong to any of us based on our behavior, ability or effort. When we try to wear it outwardly, it's at best a filthy menstrual cloth in His sight. No matter how we try to disguise self-righteousness or how fervent the mask we wear, it has an odor. We count countries and hang flags and give applause to the workers as if they are something. And by doing so, we instill self-righteousness into ourselves.

*   *   *

God's Grace shows me my depravity in its darkest, deepest hiding place and then shows me that God still loves me.

God's Grace forgives all offenses and does not demand a payment in return.

God's Grace is the only giver of hope, which is a confident expectation of victory over sin and death.

God's Grace by which I stand.

There can be no mixture of Law and God's Grace, nor works and God's Grace. No saying "I know God's Grace, but . . ." The big but that brings us back to Law. Why do people feel they need to balance God's Grace? There is no balance for it. It is extreme and outrageous. It is wonderful and marvelous. It cannot be fully understood but it can be fully experienced. It opens the door for me into the holy place so that I can commune with God.

Why do churches fight against God's Grace? They need us to work in order to build their local kingdoms. They need troops, they need armies to go forth and bring in the tithes. God's Grace would remove the power of the local clergy and give it back to God.

Can you imagine this? Your brothers and sisters would judge what you wear, eat, drink, listen to and watch, then determine whether or not you are worthy of God's favor.

I have news for them in regards to me, I have never been worthy, nor will I ever be. The greatest obstacle to love is judgment in the name of righteousness. I know why the judging happens; I have done it for many, many years. The judging happens when I think I am better than someone else. The good news is that in the midst of the churches' sins, God still can be found.

God can be found everywhere, even in ungodly places. If I make my bed in hell, He is there with me. In the darkest night, there is light. In the coldest region, there is warmth. In the deepest trials and tribulations, there is comfort. I have been designed by the Creator of all things to be a vessel of love. Nothing more, nothing less. I pray I live in my potential to be so.

*   *   *

" . . . love your enemies, bless them that curse you, do good to them that hate you, and pray for them which despitefully use you, and persecute you." (Matthew 5:44)

Day Twenty

The weather is unbelievable this evening. Eighty degrees and sunny, yet not hot. Humidity is way down. Not many clouds, just a few light ones to the west and very high in the sky. It is December twenty third and people are wishing for cooler weather. Actually complaining that it's too warm. But it feels like heaven to me. I remember the cold, the ice and the slush that lasts for months up north. The gray days that never seem to go away. I love it here. The sun shines nearly every day and it is warm and wonderful this evening. No complaints from me, only thanksgiving.

Times flies though, not a complaint just the truth. Time flies in a supersonic jet. Time is like a missile racing through the air, fast moving, and before you know it, boom!

The longing in human hearts for love is a strong desire. To be loved is the greatest thing on Earth. God has placed that desire in all our hearts. Ultimately we find love's depth in Him, and only Him. But to experience love from a human vessel to another human vessel changes lives. In both the giver and the receiver.

Family is a gift from God in that respect. But only if cultivated properly. My family has surrendered much in allowing me to love people. I must admit that at times I put others first. For their hurt I am sorry. I can't go back but I can love forward.

Airen, my wife of thirty five years, next to Jesus you are the greatest gift God has given me. You have loved me and endured me. You have walked the same path as I for a long time and words cannot explain or express how wonderful it has been being your lover, your partner, your friend. You are the kindest mother and the greatest grandmother. Allison, Ashley and Josh, you are all reflections of your mother and I. You are all like me and you are all like your mother, a blend. Being a father comes with its obstacles. No one gave me a how to book and my father didn't teach me everything I needed to know. But that's the way it is, we learn on the fly. And that learning process caused pain at times for all of us. I am so sorry for whatever pain I caused you. I love you deeply. You are a part of me. Zeke and Nate, my sons, not in-law, but in-heart, in-love, you two are the greatest husbands to my daughters. Friends to me. I love that we are close and that we enjoy each other's company. I am thankful that you love me and without you my family would not be complete. And my grandchildren. So beautiful, so unique, so special. There is no way to evaluate one better than the other. I love them all. They shine the light of God into my soul. They make me smile and laugh. They are good medicine for me.

I salute my family tonight, as I sit here watching the sun set, for loving me, for allowing me to love strangers, to take them in. We have many adopted family members connected by love. We have witnessed people change, their lives transformed by God's love. Ours transformed by them. Thank you, for allowing me to be free to be me. I love you, this Christmas, you, my family are the greatest gift.

> "And walk in love, as Christ has
> also loved us . . ." (Ephesians 5: 2)

Day Twenty One

The sunset this evening is beyond measure in beauty. The dolphins have decided to join us for a show. They seem excited and energetic in the water below my perch, here at Billy's. The air is cool again but the sun is warm. It is a great mixture. I never get tired of the colors. Each night, a new display.

Remember the song written by Pete Townsend and recorded by The Who, titled *I can see for miles*? Well God can see inside of me. He can see the deepest darkest parts of my heart. And whatever light of His that shines through me, is tainted by my flesh. That is why the Scriptures claim we see through a glass darkly. A tinted window at best. It's hard for people to see the Christ in me because my flesh obscures their view of Him.

That's why I don't study men, I study Him. I have stopped my endless reading, as if truth is found in a book, when in reality it is found in a person. I listen as He speaks, hushed by His presence. In awe.

The sound of music plays while He speaks. He's not loud, almost a whisper. But I hear Him. He speaks of unconditional, inseparable, intentional love. He assures me I will never be alone again and I will never be unloved. He speaks of His wounds and scars. He tells me how His blood has cleansed me. And He whispers, in a still small voice.

The Earth on the other hand is loud and I no longer see it as my home. This is a journey and I am a sojourner in this land. And although I know this to be true, far too often I cling to this dust. The Religion of dust has destroyed the true concept of God. It grabs hold of the Old Testament and uses Law to increase self-righteousness of man. It adds in a dash of grace and a dash of truth, though God has promised to vomit this mixture out of His mouth.

I am not referring to individual people trapped within the system, for there are many who love and share and sacrifice for others. But the system is corrupt and it has been since the beginning. We have made God into a theological discussion, as if our limited knowledge was a tower of Babel. We accept those who agree with us and believe with us, but if they disagree or challenge our belief system, we cut them out of our lives and throw them away as if they are dirty underwear. That is not love. That is cultic behavior. That is Religion.

I was born and raised a child of Rome but I couldn't fit into the system. I hated their idea of God. And while I was among those under the deception of needing a mediator other than Christ, I met some wonderful people. Even though the church tried to entrap us, love got through. God revealed Himself once again in the midst of deception and error. Then I met Jesus. Jesus broke through the religious prison I was in. It was at that moment that I believed in Him and nothing else. No one had been more loving then Him up to that time. And from that time on, He has been the most loving and the most patient and gracious towards me. That night He loved a man like me and I discovered that what I was taught was in error. He didn't want to send me to hell for what I was doing; He wanted to take me to heaven because of what He had done. So I left the Roman fold and journeyed on with Christ.

Religion being skillful in its tactics, in its power of persuasion, just like in the garden, I got trapped again. The need for a social life surfaced, the devil knew where I was weak. So I unofficially became a member of the Gathering. I always refused to sign a piece of paper for membership; I thought that was taking membership a bit far. That is why I identified myself as an unofficial member. Yet, there I found a social life, and it was good, but it was not God. Don't misunderstand me. Listen, God was there in the midst of it.

God is everywhere present. He is everywhere and if you seek Him, you will find Him. Just knock and He shall open the door. These people were dear to me. I loved them then and still do. God was about to test their allegiance to love. He was going to test the depth of their love and their understanding of His Grace. I can now look back on this test and enjoy the lesson, but at the time it hurt. God had unveiled the doctrine of eternal security to me through a dear friend. The problem was simple; the Gathering's money intake depended on that doctrine being false. Guilt and condemnation is their theme. I didn't know before the test came that I was beguiled. I could hit a softball and I could sing. I came with Airen, who doesn't love her? But come test day, I discovered they loved false doctrine more than truth. The minute I began discussing the possibility that God's Grace was even greater than we knew, I got called into the office. I was told that I was in error and my doctrine was evil. I tried to reason with the leader of the pack but his ability to study Scripture was hindered by his allegiance to headquarters. Accepting doctrine from headquarters and vomiting it up verse by verse without ever questioning its truth. The leader had become the mediator between God and man. Christ was pushed aside and ignored. I implore you to question all that you are taught and explore truth for yourself. See both sides of the coin; you need not fear as they tell you. The Holy Spirit will lead you and guide you into all truth. He promised us. He will use everything and everyone in our path. Never settle until you are drowning in God's Grace and flowing in His love.

I left the Gathering to unofficially again join another group calling themselves the Mouth of God. They had to change their name a few times. That was a sign I missed. This group was the best of the best. Religion at its finest. There were people who loved God and loved the lost. They hunted everywhere for them. They cried out to the lost. Every day, all day. They even "blitzed", hundreds converging on a city, like a flash mob, tracts in their hand and the Romans Road Plan in their mouth. God was there, but not as part of the fabric. He wasn't woven in, but separate from the Religion with its man worship and human effort called works.

God traveled in and through the deception looking for a broken heart and a wounded soul. This group studied the Scriptures, Bible College and all. I learned words like, exegesis, and isagogics. There was Greek and Hebrew everywhere. People from around the globe came to see the glory and partake in the wisdom of the so called Mouth of God. A problem arose because of the pride that ran deep in the hearts of all involved. Leadership was being exposed by God for constructing a doctrine that protected both the flesh of leadership and the flesh of the congregation. The higher you rose or the more money you gave, the more the false doctrine was used to rescue you. And if you discovered the truth, you were marked and avoided. Spoken about in whispers. Lies made up to explain the sinfulness of your departure. You had to be backslidden to leave such a place, is what they would say.

This test was about doctrine. Yet even though a hundred men from around the world gathered to correct doctrinal error, the leadership rejected the suggestions. So I left More Mercy as it was now called. Good name, but not in practice.

> "Stand fast therefore in the liberty wherewith Christ has made us free, and be not entangled again with the yoke of bondage." (Galatians 5:1)

Day Twenty Two

The sun is setting as usual, but there is nothing usual about it. Each sunset is so unusual. It is a beautiful night and it seems to release the pain from my body and soul, allowing me to breathe and rest. The colors are bold again tonight. The sunset is always more colorful when there are clouds around.

Let's go back in time. I have a child in heaven, Jimi is his name, or Angelina. Not really sure. My Airen and I got pregnant and we struggled with the decision of whether to keep our child or abort. We were young and wild and we were afraid. I know some may be appalled that we decided to abort the pregnancy. Some may call me a murderer. A religious spirit cannot find forgiveness for some sins. I even knew God at the time. Not well, but we had been introduced.

My Airen anguished over the decision. She thought God would never forgive her. So you can imagine her joy when Allison, our firstborn, came. And then we had another child, Ashley, and you would think that would erase the thought of God punishing her. But it didn't. Religion with its guilt and promise of punishment was embedded in her heart early on in life. Before the girls were born, my wife didn't believe that God would give her another child. He had to punish her, didn't He? That's what she thought. It is what she was taught. After the girls, her perceived punishment changed. Airen now believed that God would never give her a son. Interesting how guilt and punishment can be a chameleon, changing with circumstances. Why do we think such things as children of God? Has Religion caused us to turn God into an avenger? A punisher? Then Joshua came. Swoop, there he was. Joshua was a sign of forgiveness for Airen. You see, even if we fail to see the sign of forgiveness called the Cross, He sends other signs to us. He has forgiven us all at the Cross. Forever forgiven, forever forgiven. Emphasis of His Love. His love poured out in a stream of blood from the holes in His hands and side. No more guilt, no more condemnation.

"If we are faithless, He remains faithful . . ." (2 Timothy 2:13)

Day Twenty Three

The sunset tonight is breathtaking. The sky is clear and the moon, a silver crescent, is starting to rise with Venus shining brightly just above it. Most think it's just a star, but I know the truth. The sunset doesn't end when the sun melts into the horizon. It lasts for more than an hour after that. The colors intensify then fade into the night. This place is my heaven on Earth. My tabernacle. My place of communion.

The tent in the wilderness was the place where Israel depended on God for everything. Manna, quail, water. All of life's necessities. Not the temple in Jerusalem. The temple was there to feed their pride and self-righteousness. The tent in the wilderness, now that was God. The brass altar, covered in the blood of the sacrifice. The brass laver with its mirrored interior. What a lesson in approaching God. After the priest killed the sacrificial animal, he would wash his hands in the brass laver. When he approached the laver and the water, he could see his image in the mirrors below. Yet once the blood from his hands mixed with the water in the laver, the priest could no longer see his image in the mirrors; it was obscured by the mixture of blood and water. Remember the blood and water that came from His side as they pierced Him with a spear? He was telling us that He could no longer see the image of us sinners because Jesus' blood obscured His view of sin. He could no longer see it. God's altar was Calvary. The sacrifice was human. Not an animal but the Lamb of God.

From a sinner's mouth to a sinner's ear, I must ask, how can we be sure of truth that is presented to us by a man or woman who knows nothing as they ought? God's words inform, but never accuse. His words edify and encourage and never tear down. His words are love and mercy and forgiveness and Grace. His word is justification, which means seen as innocent in His eyes. His word is sanctification, which means pure and holy in His sight. His word is glorification, which means that we are equal with Him by faith. I am able to hear His words. And even if I make my bed in hell, He would be there with me.

*   *   *

Oh how I need to see with His eyes. Not marking iniquity, set free from the Law. When God numbered the years of Israel in Scripture, He never counted the times of the disobedience. He never counts mine as well. It's as if He doesn't see my backsliding. Shall I sin because His Grace does much more abound? That has already been answered,

God forbid. But sin I will. I have failed from the womb. Long before the terrible twos, I had learned how to manipulate my parents with a cry, a look, a smile.

Religion uses the words I and we, our church and our pastor. But the words that have life are these: through Him, by Him, and in Him. Not I, you, we or me. No ministry, no pastor, no pope. Only Him, personal pronoun of the highest order. When I look into the eyes of Jesus I see life. I must not allow Religion to ever again hinder my view of God. Tell me of your theology and of your exegesis of original language. Speak to me of isagogics and of the historical background. I know those words. And I know the system called Religion with its rules and regulations and manipulations. Yet God only visits our buildings made of stone to free people from the deception that Religion so skillfully teaches. He rescues them from the Law and sets them free. For if I am under the Law, my sin is in the way of my communion with Him. I need the blood of Christ to be eye salve, to heal the way I see.

*   *   *

His words are truly life, yet without the demonstration of Grace and love towards me, His words would be empty. We have all heard words, but action does speak louder than words. He has demonstrated His love towards us. While we were yet sinners, Christ died for us.

Let me ask this question, in closing out the day. How do these words display humanity? Manipulation, mutilation, murder, slavery, genocide, rape, war, pedophilia, incest. Need I go on?

> "For the time will come when they will not endure sound doctrine; but after their own lusts shall they heap to themselves teachers, having itching ears; and they shall turn away their ears from the truth, and shall be turned unto fables." (2 Timothy 4:3-4)

Day Twenty Four

I came out to my perch again tonight, braving the cold air. Brisk, yet cold by Florida standards. The sun is warm, as usual, but the cold air wins this battle of the atmosphere. The snowbirds are arriving in droves from up north; need to get here earlier to get a seat. They have put down the old vinyl windows that block the wind. It makes it hard to see clearly.

I begin to think about dirty windows. Have you ever looked through a dirty window? The view is obscured. You don't really see anything clearly. Limited knowledge can only carry you so far. That's why I know that judging is wrong. I don't even see myself with crystal clear eyes, how in God's name am I going to see you clearly?

Love is patient and kind, gentle and longsuffering. Love forgives, doesn't keep count of offenses. Mine or yours. Forgetting what is behind, I need to press on.

God's Grace is not a theological debate. God's Grace is not a license to sin. God's Grace is not a debt we owe. God's Grace is a relationship, a deep intimate relationship with Him. An inner peace. God's Grace is truly a way of life.

Better yet, it is abundant life. Not a period of time in which we occupy a body, but an exchange. An infusion of God from God.

*   *   *

Grace is God chasing me in the deepest, darkest places. Grace is God never letting go of my hand. His power keeping me from getting lost. His strength upholding me like the wind gently holds the Osprey. Strong and gentle, loving and kind. He has never let go of me and in truth He has pulled me carefully through this life.

*   *   *

God's Grace produces love. It cannot be balanced with the Law, cannot be mixed with the Law, for then it ceases to be Grace and is not of God, nor is it from God. The Law kills, but God's Grace gives life. It takes the payment due and pays it in full. How do you balance that? Grace does not fit in a religious setting, with its self-righteous attitude. It is better suited for those who know they are sinners and know they have a need.

As I think back over my life, I can see that my entire existence has been one of Grace being poured out continuously on me from God. Religion came in and clouded my view for many years. Obscured the truth by getting my focus off Him and off what He has done for me, in me and to me. Religion got me to focus on what I can do for Him. What a deception. I can do nothing for Him. I have nothing to offer. A filthy rag is my self-righteousness.

God's Grace has many subtitles. Justification, sanctification, glorification, atonement, forgiveness, mercy. It is a path of life, not a theology to be studied. A love to be embraced. Religion was formed early in the history of the church. Self just couldn't decrease so that He would increase. Mankind built huge buildings and wore glorious robes. Built altars of gold. Mankind prayed at the feet of statues and, through guilt, built a kingdom that has no resemblance to Christ. They wiped out the message of Grace delivered to Paul for this time in history and embraced the message of Peter for a kingdom to come. But the message of Grace has not gone away completely and those who fail at Religion come to see it as a salvation of sorts. For what the Law could not do through ordinances, Grace can do through love. When I get a glimpse of God's Grace, I understand that all my sins have been paid in full. I understand that no work or effort on my part can do what He has done to me and for me. I understand that service has nothing to do with His work on my behalf. God's Grace shouts from the mountaintops that

I am clean. I am pure and holy in His sight, by faith in Him. Faith alone. Nothing more, nothing less.

*   *   *

Religion keeps wanting to fellowship with my sins. It wants me to be guilty, or at least sorry. Religion wants to see some outward manifestation of works, so that I can be justified in its sight. But I am already justified in His sight by His Grace. Through faith. Religion likes my sins. It focuses on them, constantly bringing them to my attention, as if I don't already know about them. Religion wants to preach about my sin, yet if it would preach about Him instead of my sins, my focus would change from sin to Him, don't you think? The strength of sin is in the Law. If I ever hear a message about tithing, or service, or duty, or responsibility, or works, it will be too soon. It has never been about us, it has always been about Him. He created, He came, He died, He rose from the dead, He keeps those who believe in Him and He makes us like Himself. End of discussion, sleep well tonight.

*   *   *

" . . . and mercy rejoices against
judgment." (James 2:13)

Day Twenty Five

Won't be here at Billy's long tonight, the temperature is dropping fast. The cold air from the north is waging war on the south and will win this battle. I came here earlier than usual, hoping for the last rays of sun to offer some warmth. But this will pass quickly and we will see seventy degrees again soon. The sun will warm our skin again in a few days.

Much different than up north where the cold lasts for what seems like a lifetime during the winter. It feels brisk tonight; fresh, cold, but not enough to chase me away from my perch. The trees aren't dancing; they are slanting towards the south with the northern wind blowing fast and hard. It feels good. The Osprey is gliding high, held up by the power of the wind. It looks as if he is playing. He is spirited tonight, flying fast and playfully fifty feet in front of me. Sometimes he edges closer. I have always loved to stop and smell the roses. Always loved to watch the wind blow in the trees, to smell fresh cut grass. But this night is ridiculous in its beauty; cloudy and cool in both sense of the word.

I think back on how I was raised. The son of a steelworker, in a steel mill town. My father was not big, but he was strong. He was a hard man at times, I now understand why. But the whys don't help when you are young. My mother was an angel, so much love, yet sometimes with a need to hide in fear from my father. Not because he ever laid a hand on her, I don't believe he did. But because he was overpowering in opinion and thought, to the point of crushing her spirit at times. He loved her and she loved him, but I think she suffered inside at times. I know he did too. His childhood was difficult. They worked hard, both of them. They provided an education, fed, clothed and housed six children. They were great parents and for them I am thankful to this day.

When the Scriptures speak of the sins of the father being passed down to the children, I believe it speaks of genetic traits as well as learned behavior. I was a lot like my father when I was younger. Hard on the inside, hard on myself and on others. In doing so I hurt many people, even my parents. I hurt friends who trusted me. I hurt women who cared for me. I hurt my wife and children way too many times. But Christ has become water to the hardened clay that is my heart. He is softening me and teaching me that love needs a broken vessel to pass through.

*　　*　　*

Religion instilled self-righteousness in me, causing me to be a vessel of dishonor. Receiving God's Grace makes us vessels of honor and though I have not attained perfection, I press on until the journey is over for me. I cannot go back and make up for the hurt and pain I have caused. But I can redeem the time now, in the present and the future. God has made it possible for me to re-write my future. And for that I am eternally grateful.

*　　*　　*

"But we have this treasure in earthen vessels, that the excellency of the power may be of God, and not of us." (2 Corinthians 4:7)

Day Twenty Six

I know that sunsets are wonderful sights all over the Earth, yet this place is where God has been meeting me, teaching me. It is my favorite spot on Earth and it is beautiful every evening. Tierra Verde, Florida. Billy's rooftop bar. You need to see it. Not only beautiful, but peaceful. Tonight the sun is casting a pink hue to the sky. The clouds look like giant pillows, big and puffy and white. As I sit here, I sense His love for mankind. I feel that the only thing that grieves His Spirit is people rejecting His Grace while clinging to Religion. He did it all, He finished the work. Yet men strive daily in their own efforts.

Religion is a subject I know well, I was entrapped for nearly fifty seven years in it. From birth to peace. Has been a long time. Religion cannot exist without boasting in itself and its works. It applauds its own service and, better yet, its obedience. Don't misunderstand me, obedience is better than disobedience. But the boasting reveals whether it is flesh or spirit. Religion boasts in itself, in its preaching, teachings, its moral living and size, in how many countries it has been in and in assigning chief seats in the assembly. Religion mixes Law into this dispensation of God's Grace, but nor is it God, neither is it His Grace. The Law weighs heavy on every heart and mind. Baptizing infants, Religion starts the deception early. The Law, which Religion loves, does not give life. On the contrary, the Law kills. Once again please do not misunderstand me, the Law is good. The Law is the character and nature of God revealed in written form. But the Law is weak because of my flesh. I cannot obey in full the requirements of the Law. I obey in measure, as all mankind does. Yet I also disobey in measure, as all mankind does. The Law simply condemns me and fills me with guilt. The Law entered the human scene so that sin would increase and so that each and every man would see that he is sinner. Equal to all sinners, regardless of measure. The strength of sin is in the Law. The more the emphasis is on sin, the less it is on God and on His Grace. Don't talk about the tithe. Preach of His obedience and what it meant to all believers. Don't talk about our obedience; that is like idolatry. Exalting human obedience with its flaws over His perfect life and sacrifice.

*   *   *

Religion works wrath in our souls through the Law. Anger, depression, loneliness, eating disorders, murder, lust, crimes, even wars. If I need proof of sin causing death, all I have to do is look at the world. Death is everywhere. The world is increasing in its violence. I am not just talking about armies and nations. I am talking about the general population waxing worse and worse. Soon violence will fill its cup. Then God will move against His enemies. But this is another place of error in the teaching of Religion. God's enemies are not human. He fights not against flesh and blood but against principalities and powers unseen by the human eye. Religion calls those who disagree with its teachings enemies. Christ calls us friends.

*   *   *

Religion has erected a barrier between God and man. That barrier is the Law. The Law doesn't have a part in this dispensation. This dispensation is called God's Grace. Religion introduces Law into the mixture to destroy intimacy between a believer and God. Religion hinders deep fellowship between a believer and God, by keeping people in the shallow end. It keeps believers from experiencing God's Grace. God's Grace is not just a definition from the Greek. It is the experience of life. To know beyond a measure of a doubt that we are forgiven of all offenses against men and God. To know in the depth of our being that He lives in us. To experience the depth of His love, the width of His love, the height of His love.

Christ obeyed the Law in every point. He dotted every I and crossed every T. He finished the work of obedience according to Law, from His birth through His death. Not once did temptation get Him and He was tempted in deeper ways then I have. He obeyed, I never have. Amazing how I think that doing well or that doing better is good enough.

Followers of Religion called for the Law in the wilderness, asked for it by saying that anything God would tell them to do, they would do. Can you see the arrogance in that statement? God gave them the Law as they requested and Religion has not let go of it since Sinai. The Law was given to those who boasted in their potential obedience. And the future proved them in arrogance. The Law was not given to be a burden or a badge of honor, but a light to see that we have fallen short. Before I leave tonight, I have this thought to close the evening with. Those who desire to be under the Law and in a Religion that mixes Law and Grace, don't they hear what the Law is saying? Guilty is the only possible verdict when being judged by a perfect Law. That is why, even today, the voice of God is heard from the heavens crying our innocence. His declaration of Grace. Just as the blood of Abel cried out from the earth and reached the ears of God, the blood of Christ cries out from the heavens. The blood of Christ screams mercy. It reaches from Calvary to now.

The Law kills and the spirit gives life, but the fruit of the spirit being love, joy, peace, selflessness, gentleness, goodness, faith, meekness and temperance, is life eternal. This is valued in the measure that we can leave the Law behind us and treasure our fellowship with God. And that is His desired intention. To fellowship with each of us. To love us. And it is His Grace that enables this fellowship to be rich.

*   *   *

Religion has various effects on mankind. Those who are better at obeying rules and regulations most often enter into pride and display arrogance. They even clothe it in a form of humility. But it looks like a filthy rag to God. Others fail so miserably at obeying rules and regulations, they enter into depression and withdrawal. They hate God, and with reason. They simply can't find Him in their religious homes and churches. And some just shrug it off like it's a myth. They listen to science which is finite, when God is not. I pray that their journeys bring them all to a divine appointment.

Why does Religion feel the need to balance Grace and truth? It doesn't give balance to our lives; it weighs heavy on us and pulls us down. Causes us to fall. Men of the cloth. Now that's a description, isn't it? Men of the cloth. They will preach about and defend men's need for obedience, not understanding that it's the goodness of God that turns us around from flesh to spirit. It's the goodness of God that leads men to a change of heart and direction. Who am I that God's hand would reach out to me? To love me? To change me? Not in an external show in the flesh, but like a potter pouring water into my heart of clay. Drowning me in His Grace. He softens me, so that the hardness of my flesh becomes useful in the hands of the potter.

*   *   *

Now obedience is a great subject. Should we? Yes. Do I? No! Can I? No! You see, I understand the measuring cup of mankind. It is as such: trying is good enough, coming short is the norm. But obedience must be free of self for it to be recognized by God, for the flesh is not recognized by God. Adam is considered the first man and Christ the second man. The first man, Adam, failed the test of love by not being obedient in the garden. He didn't trust God and I would have fared no better. The temptation was great and steady. As Adam's descendants, we too sinned in the garden, in him, in Adam. At first glance it seems unfair that I, a product of Adam's genetic seed, should be held accountable for his disobedience. But upon a closer look, I see that Christ, the second man, was obedient in His test. Even unto His death upon the cross. And the mystery revealed by Grace is that when I placed my faith in the second man, in Christ, I received His obedience on my account. I am dirtied by the first man, and cleansed by the second man.

Jesus of Nazareth, His mother scorned for being a pregnant teenager, was hated by Religion in the womb, seen as sin by the religious crowd. In the womb. That's how they referred to Him while He was still in the teenager's womb. Sin. They would all whisper behind His back, even His half brothers and sisters. Some were bold and cruel in their expression of displeasure. Religion hated Him and hates those who want only Him.

As Adam represented us in the garden, Christ not only represented us on the cross, but in death, in the courtroom of heaven, in the resurrection from the grave, and now in the throne room of heaven, where we both stand today. Clean before God. Holy, forgiven, accepted, loved. Paul said it was a mystery hidden from mankind, now revealed through him, a messenger of God's Grace. In Him. Those are great words. In Him. We are in Christ by faith, In Him and His obedience. My obedience doesn't come into play, for there is no such thing.

*   *   *

Fruit of the spirit is what mankind craves, but Religion doesn't deliver, nor can it. God's love is that fruit we desire. So deep that it can turn the other cheek, be spat upon and not be mad at the individual. His love so wide, it forgives those who tortured Him and hung Him upon a tree.

Religion tramples God's love underfoot, crushing His children. I am thankful that God is not afraid of Religion, for it cannot deceive Him. I am thankful that He ventures into their buildings made of brick and mortar. I am thankful that He walks among the deceived to get their attention. That's where He found me. I was wandering in self-righteousness, loving the applause and adulation. I pray that I am not entangled again with that yoke of bondage.

Religion is a perversion of God's Grace. Concerning Religion Paul wrote "Beware of the dogs, beware of evil workers, beware of the mutilators of flesh" (Philippians 3:2). He was referring to the Jewish believers who were polluting the gospel of Grace by mixing the Law into in. Paul said we are to have no confidence in the flesh, not even a little.

> " . . . their shepherds have caused
> them to go astray . . ." (Jeremiah
> 50:6)

Day Twenty Seven

Someone mentioned to me recently that they could not understand what writing about the sunsets had to do with God. I answered that the glory and majesty of God is revealed in His creation. Sunsets are glimpses of His power and His love.

Take tonight for instance. It's cloudy, a storm is brewing. The wind is whipping across my face and a sprinkle of rain is falling. Not enough to chase me away, but soon a downpour will cleanse the filth of earth. I see God in the creation. I hope you do as well.

I know that to some of you, upon first glance, what I write looks like heresy. That's the word Religion uses to keep truth from being examined. In my experience, I have been told numerous times not to read certain authors, for they disagreed with the teachings of the sect I was involved in. Yet truth is not afraid of examination. On the contrary, continual examination leads to life. We must learn to trust that the Holy Spirit will lead us all into truth. Let's examine the concept of two gospels, without fear.

Paul the Apostle was frowned upon by many in the beginning because of two issues. First, he wasn't one of the twelve that walked with Jesus, and second, he was teaching an entirely different message than the other twelve. In his letter to the Galatians, Paul wrote "When they saw that the gospel of the uncircumcision was committed unto me, as the gospel of the circumcision was to Peter . . . they gave to me and Barnabas the right hands of fellowship" (Galatians 2:7;9).

Two gospels, two distinct teachings, for two distinct groups of people. Same God, different dispensations. Paul continued saying "For He that had effectively worked in Peter to the Apostleship of the circumcision, the same was mighty in me towards the Gentiles. And when James, Peter, and John . . . perceived the (gospel of) Grace given unto me . . . that we should go to the heathen and they unto the circumcision" (Galatians 2:8-9).

As I said, two distinct groups of people, Circumcision {Israel}, and Uncircumcision {Gentiles}. Two distinct gospels, the gospel of the circumcision, and the gospel of the uncircumcision. The first gospel, to Israel, concerned the coming of the kingdom of God to the Earth, the thousand year reign, which is still to come. The second gospel, to the Gentiles, concerned the good news of salvation by God's

Grace alone through faith alone. Paul claimed that he had met Jesus while on his way to Damascus. He was sent by the religious leaders of Israel to arrest the Jews who believed Christ was the Messiah. Religion sent him on this mission. Paul claimed that Jesus gave unto him the revelation of a mystery that was hidden from men since the beginning of the world.

That mystery is called the gospel of Grace. The gospel of Grace not only includes the truth about Christ's death on the cross wiping out the transgressions of the whole world, but also tells of the wonderful inheritance of each and every believer. This gospel of Grace speaks of the believer having a treasure in heaven and reveals that God sees us now as being sinless and perfect in His sight. That we are now seated above in heavenly places and joint heirs with Christ. The gospel of Grace elevates the cleansed sinner into a place of acceptance and love. On the other hand the gospel given to Peter, the one concerning Israel, talks of Law and obedience, with repentance being necessary for the kingdom to come.

Peter's gospel was not accepted by many in Israel. The religion of that time refused to accept Jesus as their Messiah. It refused to admit they crucified their Savior and to this day awaits another. To this day, most in Israel reject the notion that Jesus was their Savior. On the other hand, Paul's gospel spread like wildfire across the known world. His was good news to the ears of those who desired salvation. Their sins were paid for in full by Christ's shed blood. Their sins were forgiven. They were welcomed into the family of God as joint heirs with Christ. They rejoiced in the truth that when they died and put off this flesh, they would be like Him. The gospel of Grace brought forgiveness to a Gentile world that was scorned by Israel, even to the point of calling them heathens.

In this present dispensation of Grace, God has delayed Israel's national salvation, yet made it possible for all individuals, whether Jews or Gentiles, to be united in Him. Can you see now why even the twelve that walked with Jesus had trouble with Paul's teachings?

They called Paul to Jerusalem to stand before them and give an answer for his gospel of Grace. The Jews who believed Jesus was the Messiah could not handle the ending of Law as a way of life. They could not deal with Grace. Not much has changed today. Religion still cannot fathom the heathen being accepted simply by faith. Apart from works and service. Religion still to this day preaches a gospel that includes works and service.

I am saddened to say that Paul's message of God's pure Grace did not last long, even among the Gentile world that embraced it so readily at first. The Jewish believers could not stand the message of God's Grace. The teaching of God's Grace did away with the Law in their sight and they loved the Law. Even though they couldn't keep it themselves.

They followed Paul wherever he went with his gospel of Grace and tried their best to pollute his message. They mixed Law in with Grace, but by doing so made it no longer good news. Paul tried to reason with them, saying the Law written in stone was abolished by Christ's fulfilling the Law. Paul tried to make them see that Christ, our representative, fulfilled the Law in every point and by doing so accomplished what we could not.

He tried to help them understand that Christ, who had fulfilled the Law, was willing to grant forgiveness and favor to sinners by faith alone in His work. But men have always, in their pride, wanted to do things themselves.

* * *

Paul wrote to the Galatians, who had received with joy the freedom of God's Grace by faith, but once again become entangled by the Law. He called what they now believed, another gospel. He called the Law a yoke of bondage. Religion had begun its takeover of the gospel of Grace. Even to this day, the pollution that Religion brought in during the early stages remains strong and filthy in the churches of this Earth. Some are more polluted than others, but most are defiled.

The gospel of Grace though has not been diminished in any sense of the word. On the contrary, it remains powerful to those who have ears to hear what it says. The gospel of Grace is the light that Christ spoke of. He said that Religion would hide it under a bushel basket so that it could not brighten a darkened world. Yet bushel baskets are woven and as the fabric of Religion wears on mankind, a rip in the fabric of Religion will occur at times, allowing mankind to once again perceive the Grace of God clearly.

* * *

Religion is deceptive at best. It introduces Christ with a message including a dose of His Grace, but then brings in Law with its rules and regulations to keep the congregations needy and under control. The gospel of Grace was given to Paul so that he could reveal it to us, setting us free from the bondage of Religion. It sets us free from the shadow of sin and death. It sets us free to receive love and to pour it out to others. It sets us free from condemnation and guilt when we fail.

*　　*　　*

"Christ is become of no effect unto you (who think) you are justified by the law; you are fallen from Grace." (Galatians 5:4)

Day Twenty Eight

Religion, as stated earlier, has taken the message of God's Grace and added Law to it, making it no longer good news. God calls Religion a perversion. He warned us about Religion, saying "Beware of the dogs, beware of evil workers, beware of the mutilators of the flesh" (Philippians 3:2). Mutilators of the flesh, a reference to a group called the Judaizers, who were active in their opposition of Paul and the gospel of Grace.

The silencing of the gospel of Grace started early. The Judaizers were Jews who had embraced the truth that Jesus was the Messiah. They were not a part of the early church, but a remnant in Israel. They could not see the dispensational shift taking place because of their view of the Gentiles and their love of the Law. They were not opposed to the Gentiles having faith in Christ; they just wanted the Gentiles to follow Jewish rituals and the Law.

Paul called this attempted mixture of Grace and Law another gospel, yet not a gospel at all, for Religion's message is not good news. He called the Christ that the Judaizers spoke of, another Christ. Paul warned that the mixture of Law and Grace would bewitch mankind, and it has. From then till this present day. Paul thought it perverse that the Messianic Jews would require the Gentiles to keep a Law that they themselves had never kept.

These Judaizers followed Paul everywhere and attacked his message and credentials, for he wasn't one of the twelve and hadn't walked with Jesus. Paul addressed these issues in letters to the Gentile believers, but it was not enough to keep the gospel of Grace from being polluted and ignored. That perverse gospel was an interesting mixture, which of course was not truly good news. Christ died and if you obey you get to go to heaven, if you disobey you go to hell. What power Religion held over mankind. Religion was now the vehicle of salvation. The church became the greatest tormentor of human souls. Religion burdened mankind with laws and rules and regulations. Instead of setting it free.

Religion refused to rightly divide the dispensation of Kingdom and the dispensation of Grace. It still does. We must, as individuals, rightly divide the dispensations with an eye on the transition between Kingdom and Grace, for only then will we see the preciousness of God's Grace and experience its power. No external Law written in stone can change a man into Christ likeness. It is the indwelling spirit that guides us, without condemnation, and produces an eternal change in us.

*   *   *

Men saw the power that came along with leadership
in Religion. Men began to lust after positions which would
provide them with power, adoration, applause. Leadership
also included opportunity for financial gain and soon,
Religion began to sell positions of leadership.

Religion invented itself. A system that gave rewards
to those who were submissive and obedient, and promised
punishment for those who were disobedient. Religion was
not satisfied with staying in the monstrous buildings that it
erected, so it infiltrated every aspect of life.

Most of us were raised in the midst of it. You know
what I'm saying is true. If you obey mommy you get a cookie,
but if you disobey you don't get one. How many times have I
watched as my sisters ate cookies and I was not permitted to
join in? God's Grace on the other hand, says wait! Everyone
is disobedient, not one has truly obeyed. And yet because
Christ paid for the sins of the world, everyone gets a cookie.
Can you imagine how upset those who thought they were
better became?

Religion teaches that if you are sick or poor, God
must be punishing you. Religion must always include human

obedience in the equation. Grace never does. Grace says that it is Christ's obedience that matters. It is His obedience that qualified Him to be the sacrificial lamb, offered up and accepted as full payment for the sins of the world. I owe nothing because He paid it all. I cannot say that enough. If I owe anything in return for this favor, I make it a debt. And that is what Religion has done.

Religion took over society in the early years and even claimed Peter as pope. Religion held great power over the people, even claiming that the laity were ignorant and not gifted enough to read or understand the Scriptures. Religion even put the Scriptures in Latin so that the common man could not read them. Priesthood became the voice of God. Convenient power for suppression.

Religion grew strong, even to the point of selling forgiveness, calling it indulgences. Kings feared the power of Religion, for Religion determined who went to heaven and who went to hell, and people would do anything to escape hell. Religion used kings and nations to fight wars against those who disagreed with the church's teachings. History is filled with these truths I write about, they are not hidden from the mind's eye. Just suitably ignored.

Religion has always been a money making enterprise. Even Jesus turned over the tables that belonged to the thieves in the Temple courtyard. These thieves were sanctioned by the religious leaders, who received kickbacks from them. It never changed. If you wanted wine in the early stages of Christianity, you purchased it from the monks or else condemnation. If you wanted honey, the monks had bees too.

But it was the selling of forgiveness that brought a smile to Lucifer's face. It is no different today, money locked away in building funds, while people in the pews struggle to make ends meet. Religion justifying private jets and multiple homes for members of the clergy, while preaching constantly about tithing and giving. Thousand dollar suits, while children have shoes with holes in them. Religion has always been a money making enterprise. And they will call it blessings.

*   *   *

"For the love of money is the root of all evil: which while some coveted after, they have erred from the faith . . ." (1 Timothy 6:10)

Day Twenty Nine

I t seems like it's been a long time since I have seen the sunset at Billy's. Sickness has kept me away. My sickness prompts tonight's initial thought, the frailty of mankind. We've all witnessed great feats of human strength and it amazes me how strong the human being is. How resilient. But mankind's weakness also amazes me greatly. One fresh cut on the arm mixed with a microscopic bacteria or virus can kill a human being. A car wreck or a bullet ripping through internal organs and a man is left gasping for breath. Death has many ways to set us free from the flesh.

We are weak through the flesh. We may look strong on the outside but our internal organs are fragile. I see death in my aging skin. The mirror and photographs reveal the truth. Death is working in my body. And yet life is abundant in my soul and in my spirit. For He came that I may have life and have it more abundantly.

My mind shifts for a moment toward the sunset. It is beautiful, as it always is. I see the birds have made it tonight, too many to count. They fly in formations, weaving and bobbing across the sky. The clouds, like cotton balls, dot the heavens. People at Billy's are enjoying each other's company and this beauty. A nice end to a hard day.

Let's think about unity for a moment. Unity can only be accomplished when love is present in the team, in the nation and in the heart of men. His love does not overpower or force. He calls out to us in gentleness and meekness. His desire is to fellowship with us. He enjoys the time we spend together, me listening and writing while He speaks to my spirit. His love does not recognize the flesh. He does not number the minutes, hours, days, or years that we spend operating in the flesh. All that He records of our history are our walks in the spirit.

*　　*　　*

Ishmael was sent out into the wilderness for a deep lesson concerning the flesh. Israel cut off the foreskin of their flesh in another deep lesson concerning the flesh. God even tells us that we are not to know any man after the flesh. Christ yielded to the spirit instead of the flesh at Calvary. He never uttered a word in self-defense. His face was unrecognizable because of the beatings and the scourging of whips. Another deep lesson from God. No flesh will be acknowledged by Him. All sin has been paid for and forgiven.

Why then does Religion love to focus on sin? Why does Religion see the weakness of my flesh when God will not look at it? Why does Religion want to sift through the garbage to discover some dirt it can use against us? My own thoughts condemn me, why do I need to worry about yours?

It is Religion that must be marked, identified and avoided. Not people, but Religion. Religion scatters instead of gathers; it divides families for the good of the cause. We cannot mix Law and Grace and think for a moment that it will bring life. Religion is a poison that kills the soul of humanity. God desires that I turn away from Religion and its entrapments and turn towards Him. Religion infiltrated my soul at an early age and filled me with judgmental thinking. It hindered the clarity of my fellowship with God. Cutting away from flesh's strength is a different journey for each individual, but Religion is a foreskin that must be cut off.

" . . . know no man after the flesh . . ." (2 Corinthians 5:16)

Day Thirty

The wind is coming from the south; it's perfect. I have Earth, Wind and Fire playing in my earphones as I sit and wait upon God. He is never late. Philip Bailey, Maurice White, now they can sing. *Keep Your Head to the Sky*, great song. I keep my head to the sky and I see the wonderful workings of God. Jesus, the greatest artist of all time, for without Him nothing was made. And all things were made by Him.

Humiliation is a word that teaches me much about Christ. Public humiliation is something that most of the world is uncomfortable with today. In those days, it was Rome's way of keeping peace and hindering uprisings. Public flogging, public crucifixion. Christ was humiliated, stripped of all clothing and crucified naked. Beaten so badly, His own mother couldn't recognize His face. So much bleeding as He approached the hill. His skin was raw from the cat-o-nine tails.

Someone else had to carry His cross the last steps. They didn't think He would make it this far. But His love for mankind drove Him to the end. All that was left now was for them to nail Him to a beam and lift it into place. The words uttered at that hour by Jesus are life changing "Father forgive them, they know not what they do" (Luke 23:34).

*   *   *

"And being found in fashion as a man, He humbled himself, and became obedient unto death, even the death of the cross." (Philippians 2:8)

Day Thirty One

The sun is setting later each evening as we head into spring. I get to sit here longer. There is so much to think about, so much to ponder. It has been a long life yet it has passed quickly. And now the sun is setting. Whatever time I have left, my desire is to be filled with His love, to have Him drench me in it and overflow my cup. I live in a world full of filth, yet I find beauty. I live in a world full of hatred, yet love is present as well. I live in a world filled with noise, yet I can hear the voice of God. I long now for this time of fellowship with Him. If all my life was only a pursuit of worldly things and ambitions, I would not find rest in my soul. This is refreshing, rejuvenating. It is a pearl of great price. I love the birds that are here every night to fish, to feed. It is wonderful to watch them as they entertain us with their beauty and grace.

Remember the story of the prodigal son? The younger son insulted the father, took what was to be his portion of the inheritance and left home. He wounded his father's heart. The father was not angry, just deeply hurt. And although the younger son crushed and grieved his father's heart, his actions could not change the love his father had for him. The father's love never wavered. Not for a moment. So the younger son goes to Las Vegas and blows all of his inheritance quickly, ending up homeless, wandering the streets. He has no friends in Vegas; no one is friendly when you are broke. He thinks back about his father's house while begging for a meal. He remembers sitting by the fire on a cold night, laughing with his father and brother. He remembers always being readily filled when hungry and thinks to himself that even the servants in his father's house had more than enough to eat and a warm bed to sleep in. He decides to go home and ask his father if he could be a servant. And so he sets off for home.

Now at this same time, the father was standing on the front porch at home, thinking of his younger son. Longing for the day when he would return. He did this every day. Stood and watched and longed in his heart to see his son again.

Then one evening the father saw a man approaching from afar. He knew right away it was his younger son. His heart exploded in joy and love. The son also saw his father, but was a little confused because his father should be in the fields at that time of day. The younger son's heart began to fill with mixed emotions. Love, joy, fear, guilt, truly a heart in turmoil, revealing that he never really knew his father's heart towards him.

As they near each other the younger son slows a bit, guilt and shame making him fearful of what the father might say or do. The father though increases speed with each step and as he gets to his son, he grabs him and hugs him, tears of joy and thanksgiving rolling down his face. The son says something about being a servant, but the father is already in motion, calling out to his servants and to his elder son to prepare a feast and to bring the robe and the ring. The father may have heard the son's request to be a servant but he would not recognize a statement from the flesh. You see flesh likes to serve, but the father is thinking of a deeper relationship, one where spirit communes with spirit. He wants his son back, he doesn't want another servant. The father took him back as an equal, nothing to be earned or worked for, no service required. The father demonstrated his love, his compassion, his forgiveness and grace. He forgave the son all without a question of where he had been and what he had been doing. The father did not mention sin at all, not once, either in word or in action. Not even a facial expression of disappointment.

Now the elder son, who took over running the family business because his father did nothing but sit on the porch and long for the return of the younger son, this elder son served, and served some more. He was good at it, always trying to get the attention of the father. He wanted the father to be proud of him, to notice his work. He thought he wasn't loved as much as the younger son whom the father longed for and spoke about so often. So how do you think the elder son reacted when the younger son was welcomed back with a feast and equal status in the family, including another portion of the inheritance? This is what he said to the father in an angry tone: your younger son who took his share of the inheritance and wasted it on gambling and lap dances comes home after blowing it all and you welcome him back and give him one third of what I worked hard to secure for you? He didn't have to say it wasn't fair, both he and the father knew that it wasn't fair, but God's Grace was being revealed and God's Grace is not fair. Thank God.

Now follow me, the younger son couldn't get the idea of service out of his mind. He felt he owed the father something. He began to serve and work for his father's love and acceptance. He could have enjoyed the benefits of sonship but his guilt and desire to work wouldn't permit him to rest in the father's gift to him. The elder son could not accept the younger son getting away with breaking the Law of God and not getting punished.

Do you see it? The younger son is the body of Christ. The elder son is Israel. Israel was having trouble allowing the Gentiles to be equal in the eyes of God. These heathens who lived a life of sin could not be welcomed into the family of

God by Grace, they needed to work and serve and prove they were worthy through their effort and obedience. Can't you hear the Jewish men gathered on the street corner saying: we have served God all this time, all these years and you're telling me that God wants to bless these filthy Gentiles with a salvation that requires no obedience to rules and laws? So everywhere Paul went with the gospel of Grace, the elder son followed in his footsteps and destroyed his work by sowing seeds of discord and doubt. The elder son was convinced that Paul's message was a lie. The elder son was so efficient in his work that even Paul's closest friends were swayed for a short while. The gospel of Grace was under attack, the enemy was service and work. There was no way in the elder son's mind that the Messiah would ever want these unclean Gentiles to be in the family, let alone without obedience to the Law.

And so the gospel of Grace became polluted from the early stages and today the church is filled with Law and works and service. This is not what God intended. The younger son, the body of Christ, is caught up in guilt manipulation with works and service, trying to please God and win a reward. The elder son is so jealous that he can't see how wonderful God's Grace is.

In every form of Religion and in every congregation, there are both younger and elder sons. There are younger sons who are so busy working and serving that they cannot see they are sons with whom the father wants to fellowship with in rest. And there are elder sons who judge the younger sons because of their past or present life choices. Only God's Grace and the love of the father can heal both men. Only when we see the action of the father and the words from his heart will we see God. "My son whom was dead, is alive again. He was lost and now he is found. Bring the fatted calf; bring the robe that represents family, and the ring that represents sonship and inheritance. My son is home where he belongs" (Luke 15:11-14).

Only when we look away from our service and our works can we see clearly the father's embrace of the sinner and the father's tears of joy. Only when we stop speaking of what we have done for the father can we hear the father say I love you, not what you do, but you, whether good or bad. Only then can we join in the father's joy and experience in full the love of the father towards both sons.

> "And (that I may) be found in Him,
> not having my own righteousness,
> which is of the law, but that which
> is through the faith of Christ, the
> righteousness which is of God by
> faith." (Philippians 3:9)

Day Thirty Two

You would think that by now I would have grown weary of watching the sun set. That I would have become accustomed to the beauty after all these days. But I cannot get enough. It's as if I am drawn to this place, to this theater, to observe the manifested glory of God. The trees, the clouds, the breeze, the birds, the sun, all working together to declare the truth. The truth that He is.

*   *   *

There is nothing wrong with the church, the body of Christ. But Religion which lies within the church, hidden in the shadows and lifted up in honor, hinders God's glory from being manifested to the world. Religion which oozes with corruption is an infection which permeates all mankind. Corruption is found in all sects and assemblies and within each and every man, woman and child. All have sinned and have come short of the glory of God. Religion, hidden deep in the heart of the church, in every heart, is the good side of the flesh. We can obey in measure and in degrees, but we can never reach the height of holiness. We are always a degree, or three, or five from perfect. Even on our best days.

Yet mankind will keep on striving and serving self. Martha, Martha you are anxious for much.

The focus of believers cannot be on my sins or on the sins of others. The focus must be God. Not the work done in His name, nor the service that is preached about so often. The focus must be Christ. I want my eyes on Him. I want my ears to hear what He says and I want to see people the way He sees people. All of them. Each and every one that I pass on this journey home. I never thought before that Christ surrendered Himself to both the hatred of humanity and the justice of God. His love was stronger than mankind's hatred. His life was a pure acceptable sacrifice. All throughout His agony, love poured out of His eyes and out of every wound. Love for His mother, for John, for Martha and Mary, for all of us, for me and you, and even for those who crucified Him. Father forgive them, they know not what they do.

It is this love, the love of God for mankind, that God calls the first love. For it was He who first loved us, long before we fell in love with Him. God demonstrated His love for us on Calvary's tree while we were yet sinners. God told us that we have left our first love and are now more concerned with our love for Him than with His love for us. Once again, making ourselves the center of attention. This is the heart of Religion, elevating ourselves to a position that belongs only to God. Religion speaks about man's love for God and man's duty. Religion speaks about man's obedience, putting the obedience of Christ in a secondary position.

Leaving Religion behind is not giving up a relationship with God. Leaving Religion behind is finding a relationship with God. A relationship without a human mediator. I don't need a mediator to speak to God for me or to get messages from Him. Most self-ordained preachers are more of a curtain than a conduit. There is only one mediator between God and man. Jesus. The cloth, the collar, the robe, the tithes, the chief seats in the assemblies, they may not even be aware that they hinder the presence of God, yet they do. Religion doesn't care if we see God. Religion doesn't mind if we hunger and thirst after righteousness, as long as we go through them. Their studies, their fasts, their good works. Religion wants us to emulate the leaders. Religion cannot rest; it is a system working in every aspect of society. It disguises itself as goodness yet is rotten to its core. God tried to tell Israel that its best works of any tense, past, present or future, offered to Him for salvation, would be rejected and would be like a filthy menstrual cloth in His sight. But few listened. Then or now.

Religion teaches us how to do everything in regards to God. How to pray, how to study, how to reach out. It not only tells us how to do it, but when to do it and when not to do it.

Religion accepts certain types of clothing, music, lifestyles, but doesn't accept all people. Religion infuses Law into every fiber of mankind. Mankind is truly captive. Religion cannot live outside the community of like believers and doesn't want us to mingle with what and whom it considers unclean. Religion believes it, in spite of Him asking us to love our enemies and to do good to those who despitefully use us.

I know that many have lives much harder than mine. So many born in pain and living in anguish. Follow me here. Those of us who have suffered a little on this Earth and in this flesh will shout with joy, as those who have suffered more get a rich and healthy reward. But we will not be jealous. On the contrary, our love for our brothers and sisters will be demonstrated. On that day we will see clearly the pain and suffering of others and there will be tears of joy, not sorrow. He will wipe them away with His graciousness. His kindness will shine like the sun. Religion hates the idea of the least being the greatest, and the last being first.

*   *   *

What kind of love do we ascribe to Him? What do we think He is like? Do we believe, as Religion does, that there is a line we should not cross and if we do, God will make us suffer in order to bring us back into the fold?

We can never be snatched from His hand; we can never leave the fold. He will not leave us nor forsake us. He doesn't want us to ever suffer for anything. He is the Balm of Gilead, the Comforter. My God is a God of Grace, of forgiveness and mercy, of love. Religion calls my God, half a God. Yet it is that part of Him, this dispensation, which He is showing forth in this age. All debt paid, no service required or needed. No debt to be paid by me, a free gift. I owe nothing to God for I have nothing pure to offer Him. So I must rest in Christ. I must bathe in what He has done for me. I must enjoy and breathe in the spirit of His Grace. Let us not lift up the sins of others. Let us lift up Christ and His finished work.

*   *   *

"And I, if I be lifted up from the earth, will draw all men unto me."
(John 12:32)

Day Thirty Three

I don't have the words to describe the weather tonight, it is so beautiful. Warm and refreshing. There is a slight breeze at the moment. That's the refreshing part. Feels like heaven to me. The sky is so blue. Not a cloud in sight. I love it here.

Communion, now that really is an interesting word. Communion does not speak of a wafer, of a piece of bread, or of a cracker. It speaks of a love relationship, an interaction, intimacy. Communion for me is putting all else aside to watch the wind make the trees dance, while listening to Him. Interacting with Him, without uttering a word.

*   *   *

I have heard that the creation testifies of a creator, and that the sun, the moon, the Earth, the stars and all humanity reveal the majesty of God. Pretending He is not there will not cause Him to disappear. Every knee will bow. The Scriptures say He is love; therefore we will not bow out of fear. We will bow because of who He is and what He has accomplished for us.

*   *   *

Remember what He said to Peter: fear not. He is Grace personified, truth revealed, and love demonstrated again and again. That's who Jesus is. Look into His eyes with the mind's eye of your imagination. Barely alive on that day, beaten . . . scourged is the word. Look at His eyes, He is not afraid. On the contrary, there is a glimmer of joy, a sparkle in His eyes. He has finished the work and with a whisper barely audible to those near, He cries out "Father, forgive them" (Luke 23:34). It is then that love triumphs over hatred and mercy rejoices over judgment.

*   *   *

Picture this scene from the movie *Jesus of Nazareth* with me for a moment. Jesus was in Peter's home, teaching, loving people. Matthew, the tax collector, had heard that Peter had made a miraculous catch the night before and was determined to collect the back taxes that he owed. As Matthew was getting closer to Peter's home, he saw that a large crowd had gathered there, and by the time he walked in, his curiosity was peaking.

Now you have to understand that the Jews hated tax collectors even more than they hated the Romans who occupied their land. This intense hatred came from the fact that tax collectors were Jews working for Rome, extorting money from their own people. They were vermin and unclean in the eyes of the Jews.

As Peter saw Matthew walk in, he became upset that this unclean tax collector would just step inside, defiling his house. Jesus also saw Matthew walk in, and before Peter could act, He asked Matthew if he would have Him over for dinner at his house that evening.

Peter became irate, not only with Matthew but now also now with Jesus. You see, Peter was a good man, a hard-working man. But he was also self-righteous. He said to Jesus: You the holy one of Israel, the Messiah, would eat with the likes of this tax collector knowing what he does to your people? Jesus, with eyes pouring out love, said to Peter: I will enter into any home where I am welcome.

This was outrageous behavior for the students of the Law; they could not believe their ears. Jesus would eat with a sinner, in a sinner's house. This is Grace magnified.

So later in the day, as evening neared, Jesus set off to eat dinner with Matthew, the tax collector. His disciples had tried to talk Him out of doing this unclean act all afternoon, but all Jesus would answer was, why don't you join us? The disciples were frustrated, but knowing He was different, special, they followed Him to Matthew's home. Yet, not daring to go in, they waited at the door. Now Matthew, after leaving Peter's home that morning, had invited quite a few guests to his home for that evening meal. Sinners like him, for the self-righteous would have nothing to do with Matthew. He was seen as unclean, one to be marked and avoided.

Peter was watching from the doorway, listening as Jesus stood to speak. Jesus told the story of the prodigal son and that story pierced the hearts of both Matthew and Peter. For Matthew represented the younger son, ignoring his relationship with the father because of sin and guilt, while Peter represented the elder son, having no real relationship with the father because of self-righteousness.

Peter, recognizing himself in the story, entered Matthew's home and approached Jesus gently. Softly he said, Master forgive me, for I am a stupid man. Unconditional love captured the hearts of both Matthew and Peter that evening. They were never the same after that.

And, once more, picture this. Jesus was teaching in the outer court of the temple in Jerusalem, the only place in the temple where the common man was permitted to be. The religious system of the day had created a couple of monsters and had called them Pharisees and scribes. They both were watching Jesus closely, looking for a reason to accuse Him of something. There was a crowd at the temple. It was the Sabbath so all good Jews were to be there. There was also a man, blind since birth, waiting by the pool, waiting to be healed.

The belief was that the first one in the pool after the waters had been stirred by an angel would receive a healing. Don't know if it was true or not but it's what they believed, so it was true to them. He, being blind, was never able to be first. But he was always there, always waiting, always hoping.

On that day, with Religion watching Him, Jesus took some dirt in His hand and spit in it, creating mud. He then rubbed it in the blind man's eyes. He told the blind man to wash in the pool and as he did a miracle happened. The man began to see for the first time in his life. He was elated beyond measure. And instead of being overwhelmed with joy for this man, the Pharisees asked Jesus why He did this on the Sabbath, breaking the Law. They accused Him of sin for healing on the Sabbath.

Picture this with me. The scribes and the Pharisees with their robes and phylacteries, those ribbons and sashes embroidered in the robes, proclaiming their good works, angry over a healing. This group of Law enforcers commanded the crowd to stop listening to Jesus, for they claimed Him to be a sinner and if anyone followed His example, they too would be in danger of hell. They tried their best to show forth their devotion to the Law, but in truth their flesh is all that was seen. The people knew, they had known for a long time, yet the people feared the consequences of going against Religion. They had just witnessed a man who was not afraid and hope ignited in their hearts.

On this day, sight was given to all the people who were blinded by the Law. Grace was revealed in the form of mercy and kindness. The Law blinds us to the beauty of God's Grace. For most, grace is a word that we exegete and study. But it is truly a life to be lived. A life of receiving and giving love in its highest degree.

*   *   *

The tablets of stone are in the way, just as the curtains in the tabernacle separate us from Him. But He has torn that curtain in two. From top to bottom. He has fulfilled the Law, taking it out of the way.

I have access by the blood. I don't have works to offer, but I have His blood on me.

I don't have service to speak of, but I have his blood on me.

Where Religion shouts obedience, the blood of Christ cries out on behalf of this sinner. I rest in that proclamation from the seat of mercy.

*   *   *

"Neither by the blood of goats and calves, but by his own blood he entered in once into the holy place, having obtained eternal redemption for us." (Hebrew 9:12)

Day Thirty Four

Another evening and the sunset is breathtaking. Music is playing in my ears and my soul is dancing with joy. I am again aware of His presence and I am in awe. It is at times like this that I realize my busy days sometimes keep me from seeing the beauty of creation. Truly, I need to stop and smell the roses more often.

This evening I am thinking of the last supper. The night Jesus was arrested and brought before the Sanhedrin, the ruling powers of Religion in Israel. I believe that Judas Iscariot revealed Jesus' whereabouts that night because he was growing more and more frustrated with what he perceived as slowness in Jesus to proclaim Himself the king of Israel and bring about victory over Israel's enemies. Especially over Rome. You see, Judas was a Jew who loved Israel. He was a zealot, a member of a group that wanted to wage a revolutionary war against Rome. He had studied the Scriptures concerning the king that was to come and lead Israel to victory and he believed Jesus was that king. Judas knew that the man with the power to heal lepers and to raise the dead was that promised king. Judas knew that the man who sickness and death obeyed could lead the nation of Israel into the kingdom that was promised.

As the feast day arrived and Jesus and the twelve entered the city to cries of Hosanna and shouts of Christ being the awaited Messiah, Judas realized that the people were behind Jesus. Judas did not care whether the Pharisees or scribes were on board or not; he had realized that they had sold their souls to Rome long ago. And Judas was hungry for the deliverance of Israel; he was a very devout man. He couldn't understand why Christ spoke of His death, none of them did. They simply dismissed the thought quickly.

So Judas decided to force His hand. He decided he would inform the Sanhedrin where to find Him. Jesus even told him to do what he must and to do it quickly. At that point, Judas believed in his heart that Jesus would rise up and confront the religious leaders of Israel and expose them as frauds. Soon Christ would be crowned king and bring peace to Israel.

The Scriptures say the devil entered into Judas. I can relate to temptation and failure. I can relate to the devil whispering in my ear and to giving heed to him. So I cannot judge Judas. It appears that Judas had a love for money. This also factored into his actions, but I do not believe money was the motivating factor for his actions.

Christ had a different path to follow in order to bring about salvation to the world; He was not to be crowned king at this time. He was to die.

I don't believe Judas could understand this at all. I don't believe anybody knew the plan. When Judas realized that his plan was not going to work, that Jesus was not defending Himself and would surely die, he went out in misery and remorse, and hung himself.

He did not understand the love of God with its forgiveness and mercy. At that point Judas found nothing worth living for; he knew that Jesus was the messiah. He knew that Jesus was the one who was promised. And now Jesus was going to be crucified and the hope for Israel's deliverance was no longer alive in Judas' mind. Judas had lost all hope. Little did he know that the death, burial and resurrection of Jesus would bring about salvation to the world. And deliverance from sin and death.

> "Hope deferred makes the heart sick . . ." (Proverbs 13:12)

> " . . . Christ in you, the hope of glory." (Colossians 1:27)

Day Thirty Five

I have been doused with God's Grace so many times in my life, I'm soaking wet. He's going to drown me in His Grace.

It is a wonderful experience having God pull back the curtain, exposing the Wizard of Oz that we call Religion, allowing me to look away from self and from others in order to see Him. That is the freedom He promised. Freedom from guilt, from comparing ourselves to others, from others comparing themselves to us. Freedom from work and effort to show our goodness. You shall know the truth and the truth shall set you free. The truth is not a doctrine, it is a person and He is living and loving through the dispensation of Grace.

*   *   *

Because of the teachings of Religion, which is a works oriented program of deceit, people today measure themselves in degrees. Most feel they are doing quite well. They hang their salvation upon it. They wear phylacteries of modern day Religion. Instead of displaying embroideries on their robes, they parade on Facebook or on other social media sites. They speak of their fasts and prayers. They tell us how long they have studied. Religion hangs flags and holds conventions. Religion measures sin in degrees too, thinking mortal is worse than venial. They preach from the pulpits what we have done and what we are going to do for God. Pastors and teachers preach works without even knowing it.

A pastor is a gift from God, but too many have sought after the title and power that comes with it. Too many have been ordained of men and not of God. Too many today trample underfoot the body of Christ by focusing on work, power and wealth. A pastor is a gift, not a title; a pastor is a friend who speaks of Christ, who doesn't build his own kingdom but points to what is finished. The deception of Religion is clearly seen when compared to the Grace and love of God. Religion, with its factions and divisions, its arrogance, power and greed, is not a way of life. It is death. Religion holds the hope of heaven hostage, making it a prize that comes through them and that must either be purchased or earned. Religion points to the work, and the work becomes the first love. In Religion, the effort is applauded and with each clap self-righteousness is fed.

*   *   *

"Take heed that you do not your alms before men, to be seen of them . . . do not sound a trumpet before you, as the hypocrites do in the synagogues and in the streets, that they may have glory of men . . . for they love to pray (openly) . . . to be seen of men." (Matthew 6:1-2-5)

Day Thirty Six

The sun feels good on my skin. I welcome the warmth. Tonight, as I sit here watching the birds flying overhead and the clouds that look like big marshmallows in the blue sky, I think of being a vessel.

We are earthen vessels made of clay, but oh how we love our pottery. Paul the Apostle brought to us the gospel of Grace. It was given to him by a risen, resurrected and seated above Christ. Grace is the new wine, yet we continue to put it in the old wineskin called Religion. Religion hides flesh in a disguise of goodness, which really is just self-righteousness. The earthen vessel must be broken, must be emptied of self, so that the life poured out is Christ.

*   *   *

Religion offers its work to God as a sacrifice. It offers its effort in order to please God, when all the while God is already pleased with the work of His Son on our behalf. God will not accept the offer from Religion since Christ already finished the work. There is a fine line that we walk, a path if you will. On the one hand, we must see ourselves totally forgiven and totally cleansed, made holy even, seated above with God. On the other hand we must not lose sight of who we are in the flesh. We must not let the finished work blind us from truth, but instead we must let it reveal truth to us. Yet we must look at ourselves with no condemnation, knowing our debt is paid and our sins forgiven. We must not act as if our flesh is not around. Imposing that lie would keep us from understanding the truth that Christ spoke of when He said that he that has been forgiven much loves much. There is no condemnation for those in Christ Jesus.

> "But we have this treasure in
> earthen vessels, that the excellency
> of the power may be of God, and
> not of us." (2 Corinthians 4:7)

Day Thirty Seven

The breeze feels cool after this hot January week. It seems that when I take time to smell the roses, life is good. The colors of creation, all so beautiful, all so unique.

The Osprey just flew fast overhead then seemed to stop mid-air, ruffling his wings in some crazy movement. He slowed down, appeared to be sizing up something, then raced back up to speed quickly. And I discovered that this Osprey is a she, not a he as I've been referring to all along. A mother with a nest, getting ready to give birth soon. She's protecting the future home of her young. That's why she is here every night.

It's nice out tonight; the sun is warm and the breeze is refreshing. God is on His throne, and all is well with my soul.

We are not some test; we are not God's science project. What we are experiencing are the consequences of sin. God desires that no man perish, so He waits for time. Time that was established in eternity past to play out, or run out, as it is. Time for all of mankind that He foreknew and foreordained to come into existence. His love will not end time early to save a few when He desires all. He will not end the consequences of sin to take place on this Earth until all those who are to be born come forth from the womb. Yet, now in time, He has freed us from the dust and has given us hope in this place of insanity. He is a light in this darkness. Time will end and the body will be filled. Until then we have faith.

Now He desires that we be vessels of honor, loving one another as He loved us and gave His life for us. Not word driven, not ordered by a commandment, but enticed by His love. Drawn to Him so that He can fill our souls with His overflowing love. Every fiber of our being, filled with the love of God.

*   *   *

We can only feel God's love when we take our eyes off the work, off the people and the Law, and place them full on Him. Only when we are able to do that, can we feel His overflowing love. The remarkable result of fellowshipping with Him. We look unto Him; we look unto who He is and what He has done. We no longer look at the work or at the service, at the tithe, at a building or at a pastor. We no longer look in the mirror. We look unto Him.

For a child of God, even politics is a distraction. We spend too much time speaking about our country and its problems, all the while thinking someone will rise up and save us from ourselves. We look to a certain politician or party, thinking the tallest, strongest or smartest will rise up and save us from ourselves. Israel did that with Saul. It didn't turn out to well for them.

God's Grace is so enjoyable. No stress, no time, just the present moment with Him. No condemnation, no talking about sin, no guilt. It's not because I haven't sinned; volumes could be written about the sins of my past, present and future. But Jesus' blood has guaranteed that those books will never be written or read. His blood has covered my transgressions. He said once that at the time of judgment, when He sees the blood, He will pass over me. I believe Him.

The blood of Jesus, the innocent man, blotting out the guilty transgressions of mankind. He, the propitiation of our sins. A finished work, once and for all. I cannot comprehend the height and depth of His love for me, I cannot figure out why He would love me, but tonight, through the tears,

I know it, I believe it with every beat of my heart, and with every breath I take.

*   *   *

" . . . Unto Him that loved us, and washed us from our sins in His own blood." (Revelation 1:5)

Day Thirty Eight

Tonight I have a new viewpoint. I'm not at Billy's; I'm seated at the bar of The Island Grill, a wonderful restaurant on the island of Tierra Verde, Florida. Great food, better people, from the owners to the cooks to the wait staff. All friendly. Tonight instead of watching the sun set and learning from nature, I sit and watch people live out their lives. Some are filled with joy, laughing, having a great time with friends. A few have confusion on their faces and pain in the eyes. They either haven't learned how to hide the pain like most do, or feel it so profoundly that they simply cannot hide it. We have all had days like that. Another few look so lonely; they seem to be seeking out a kind word, a minute of conversation. It's the responsibility of love to say something to them. I like this perch as well, for learning about humanity is a lifelong lesson. Observation is a powerful learning tool.

Tonight, as I sit here eating linguini and clams, thoughts of the fire come back to me. That's what I have called it for years. The fire. I don't remember all the players, even though I was in the game. I remember Susie, I loved her. She loved me as well; we were living together in Las Vegas. A group of friends met one night for a party at the Moby Grape, a great bar not far from the UNLV campus. Fifty-cent shots of tequila, Cuervo Gold, the party was on. We drank, we danced, we popped a few Quaaludes. Too many in hindsight. Party started early, we closed the place. As usual. Then we proceeded back to my place. Didn't even know all the people who came along but they were all welcome. Things like that never change, all are welcome. We drank some more, smoked a few and as I was slowing down, feeling ready for bed, I invited all to stay, to find a sofa or grab a spot on the floor. No need for an accident on the road. Susie and I retired from the party and went to our room. A short time later, we both passed out. I cannot tell you for sure who left, like I said I didn't know them all. But later that night I discovered who stayed. David Borkowski stayed, Susie's friend stayed, can't remember her name after thirty seven years. And a girl named Sheryl Irby stayed. I will never forget her or her name. As I was saying earlier, I had passed out from all the drinking and drugs. Anyone who has experienced that type of partying knows that when you pass out, you don't wake up for hours. Yet a few hours later I woke, clear headed and lucid. Ready to move. How can that happen in such circumstance unless it's a miracle? I heard a voice and a banging noise. It was David, screaming for us to wake up. I went to the bedroom door and opened it; David was on all fours crawling away from my door. Smoke had filled the house and the only space clear of it was the floor. From the ceiling to about three feet from the floor, the smoke was thick. It was a dark smoke yet the living room ahead of me appeared to be glowing. I wasn't ready for what happened next; it seemed to be happening in slow motion. David was in front of me, I hadn't started to move up the hall yet because I needed to wake Susie up. I saw David reach the front door and turn the handle to open it. Oxygen instantly raced into the living room, feeding the sofa that had been smoldering for who knows how long. The room exploded in flame, not flames but one huge ball of flame. The force of it threw David from the house and the flame was now racing down the hall towards me. I wish I could say I was courageous, but I panicked in fear. I freaked. Yet quick like a cat, no more slow motion, I got up off the floor and ran into my room closing the door behind me, creating a barrier between the flame and us. Susie was still asleep, passed out. Smoke was filling the room and I was standing up in the midst of it. I knew there was a window but I had lost my sense of direction and couldn't see a thing except a glow under the door. I grabbed Susie and threw her hard against a wall. Seems violent now but I didn't have much time and I didn't like the thought of dying just then. She awoke, dazed and pissed. She was awesome, I loved her. She quickly realized what was happening. I began banging on the walls with my fists looking to break open the window, if only I could locate it. I found it, it shattered, my hands ripped open from the broken glass. Susie and I jumped out of the second story window. Alive, safe, hoping everyone made it out as we did. We walked around to the front of the building, looking to see if everyone had made it out. That's when I saw Sheryl. I vomited from the sickness in my heart and body. It's hard to describe what I saw. Charcoal, severely burnt, body blackened, split open in places. The white of her eyes staring out at us. She was still alive, trying to breathe; she looked at me and me at her. She was begging with her eyes, I never felt so helpless. I watched her die and I will never forget her. I had met her earlier at the bar. She had life in her, loved to dance, beautiful beyond measure. We spoke a lot that evening, soul to soul. She had depth. She was a flirt like me, I liked her. She came back to my house and fell asleep on the couch in the living room smoking a cigarette. The couch smoldered for a while as she slept there, passed out from too much partying. David told me she came out after the room exploded in flames and a neighbor threw her to the ground to put out the fire that was on her. I will never forget Sheryl, or Susie and David. I will never forget that God woke me up. Whether He used David or whether it was God's voice that I heard. The fire, that's all I can call it.

> " . . . we went through fire . . . but
> You brought us out . . ." (Psalm
> 66:12)

Day Thirty Nine

How high can the indwelling spirit lift us up? How far will we let God take us? To what depth? And if we are hindered, it is not by sin but by guilt. Sin has been dealt with and removed. Once purified by faith we should have no more guilt or condemnation. Guilt has led many to claim they don't believe. That's one way of absolving ourselves. But it doesn't work. The concept of no God keeps me hidden from Him, like Adam and Eve in the garden.

The creation itself testifies of His glory and existence. Guilt is the problem. Guilt is the enemy of God's Grace. Religion has learned to use that guilt against us, causing countless millions to give, to go and to serve, all in the name of being well pleasing to God. Yet our attempts at being righteous fall short every time. There is not one time that we have done good. If something good happens to people, if they are blessed, it is God doing the work in them, through them and to them.

*   *   *

Understand that goodness is not a relative term in Scripture. Goodness speaks of perfection and pure holiness. It has no blemish or stain. Only Christ can claim a life lived in goodness. Only Christ is good. All others have fallen short. All others. There is none good except Jesus.

*   *   *

Christ Jesus is pleasing to God and we are hidden in Him. By faith in His work, by faith in Him, we are made righteous. He calls it the gift of His Grace. There are no other ways for us to be seated above in heavenly places. It's all through Him, by Him, and because of Him. Nothing man has to offer is of any value. We are vessels, clay pots, instruments of the Most High God. When life, with its circumstances and consequences, break us, His love pours in and out of us.

*   *   *

A closer look and I see that all that humanity is, attains, discovers and considers good or bad, is corrupt. Defiled somehow, someway. Fallen is the correct word to use. Humanity possesses a flesh nature that wars against the spirit and that is capable of the most demonic activities. And in disguise, is capable of good works. Yet totally depraved.

The deception lies in thinking that what we have to offer is somehow accepted by Him. Our goodness, the best we have to offer Him, is but a filthy menstrual cloth in His sight. A stench rising up in His nostrils. And yet, we humans still boast in what we have done and accomplished. Oh yes, I forgot. We do it in the name of Jesus.

The deception lies in thinking that we are good or better than others. That somehow, because we are not like them, we are better than them. Yet all of humanity is classified as sinners before we become saints.

The truth revolves around who Jesus is and what Jesus has done, or better yet has finished. It also involves where He is. He rose from the Earth, lifted up in a cloud of angels. He humbled Himself; God left heaven and became a man, Emmanuel. He is the new creation. God and man in one, woven together. Not a fallen man like Adam, but a second man if you will. The first man, Adam, brought death. The second man, Jesus, gave eternal life. He is now seated in heaven, welcoming home those whom death has released. He is seated above and we are hidden in Him, seated above with Him. The declaration of truth from God's mouth seals the deal for all eternity.

*   *   *

He was the Ark of the Covenant carrying the Law, the provision and the authority. He was the candlestick in the Temple bringing forth the light of the world. He was the lamb slaughtered on God's altar for sin. He was the sweet aroma of incense rising into God's nostrils. He was the Priest offering Himself to God.

*   *   *

Therefore it's not about our titles or our buildings. It's not about our preaching, our abilities or our gifts. It's not about our pastors or our tithes. It is about Him. It's about His heart of Grace, pouring out blessings the mind can only see through a glass darkly. It's about Him making us like Himself. That's why we are told to look unto Jesus the author and finisher of our faith. It's about Him.

*   *   *

I no longer want to hear about my work, my title, my service or my sin. I want to hear about Him. Tell me who He was, tell me what He did. Tell me what He said and how He healed and loved. Even unto His death. Somebody speak to me about His kindness, His patience, His compassion.

*   *   *

It's about Him. Tell me about when He was with you on this wilderness journey. Tell me how He has provided for you, time and time again. Tell me about the time when you hurt your back and could not work. You had a wife and a small child. You found money in the van, put by someone sent by Him. Tell me about the knock at the door and the bags of food left by those He sent. Don't know who they were but they were vessels of honor in my mind. I knew God sent them, I knew He loved me.

They beat the shit out of Him, tortured Him for hours. Spit on Him, scourged Him. Tore the flesh off His bones without hitting an internal organ. The Romans were skilled at their craft. They nailed Him to a tree. And what did He say? "Father forgive them, they know not what they do" (Luke 23:34).

*   *   *

The Law. The Ten Commandments written in stone. No one could obey them. They were not given so that we would obey them. They were given because man wanted Religion. They were given to show us that we could not obey them. They were given to cause sin to increase. Look it up, search the Scriptures to see if what I write is true.

After leading the Israelites out of Egypt, the land of bondage, God brought them to Sinai and told them what He had done for them. He was proclaiming His Grace. They had complained the entire journey, but God still gave them water and manna from heaven itself. So God brings them to Himself at Sinai and here is what He said: "This shall you say to the house of Jacob, and tell the children of Israel you have seen what *I have done* to the Egyptians and how *I carried you* on eagles wings and brought you unto myself" (Exodus 19:3-4). God was giving them a choice between Religion and Him. Here comes the test, as God continues: "If you will obey my voice and keep my covenant, then you shall be a peculiar treasure unto me above all people" (Exodus 19:5). Moses calls the people together and repeats what God had said. And all the people said "All that the Lord has spoken *we will do.*" (Exodus 19:8). Oh, If only they would have screamed "Lord, we cannot obey you in all that you say. The best we have to offer is tainted effort. We have complained and whispered the entire journey, please Lord give us more Grace."

We too on this journey must choose between what God has done for us and what we can do for God. There are no middle grounds on this subject; it's either all Grace or all a menstrual cloth. I understand service, I understand good works, but we have nothing to do with good works or service. If God, through the indwelling Spirit, illuminates or motivates a service or some good work in me, then it is no longer I who liveth but He that liveth in me. So where is the boasting then?

What great words these are: "If Abraham were justified by works, he has the appearance of glory, but not in God's sight, only in man's sight" (Romans 4:2). Abraham believed God, and his faith is counted as righteousness. Those who work feel the reward is not given by God's Grace. The reward is a debt, something they feel they owe in return of Grace. But those who work not, those who cease from works and rest in Christ and in Christ's work on the cross, those who believe in Him who justifies the ungodly, hold a faith that is counted as righteousness. David described the blessedness of the man unto whom God imputes righteousness without works as such: "Blessed are they whose iniquities are forgiven and whose sins are covered, blessed is the man to whom the Lord will not impute sin" (Psalms 32:2).

*   *   *

Imputation. A wonderful biblical word. The notion of charging something to someone's account. A legal word, an accounting word. Adam's sin in the garden was imputed to all mankind by God. God charged Adams sin to the account of all who came from Adam. Is it fair, you ask? But who wants fair? I do not want to get what I deserve concerning my works. God charged Adam's sin to us all, for we all have sinned *In Adam*. But God, who is rich in mercy, sent a second man, a man not born of Adam's seed, therefore free from sin even in the nature of sin. This second man lived a holy life, a righteous life. He then offered Himself and His sinless life to God. On our behalf. The Lamb of God that takes away the sin of the world. God accepted the offer and the sacrificial lamb was slain, shedding His blood for the remission of sin. Adam, the first man, represented us all in the garden when he sinned and his sin was charged to our account. Christ, the second and final man, represented us all when He obeyed the Father's will in all things. He being a spotless lamb, His account read as righteous, clean, whole. And God imputed Christ's righteousness to our account, He imputes Christ's righteousness to us all and we are now like Christ. Imputation. A wonderful word.

*   *   *

"... but sin is not imputed when there is no Law." (Romans 5:13)

Day Forty

The sunset tonight is breathtaking. It's as if God painted this one special for our last night here at Billy's. The air is cool and refreshing. The colors are exploding in front of me as they change from one moment to the next. The sun is big and bright and feels warm on my skin. It has been a wonderful journey for me. Healing in many ways.

The birds are all here tonight. The egrets, the ospreys, the seagulls and the herons. All fishing, looking for a meal. That's why I come here as well. To be fed by God. And He has given me a feast.

I have tried to convey our heart conversations to you, so that you may enjoy the feast, as I have. I hope it has been filling and nourishing to your soul. As the sun sets tonight, it sets on these writings, bringing this book to a close. But before we finish, here is a last thought.

God would not have sent His Son to die for me, if He did not love me with a deep, radical, extreme love. Calvary was an extreme demonstration of His love for all men. He calls to us all, each one equally important to Him. Each one created to fellowship with Him, in love. For God so loves the world that He gave His only begotten son. Quite a thought. Requires a moment of reflection deep in the soul.

*　　*　　*

He speaks to us all in a still small voice. A whisper that is often drowned out by the noise in our lives. Come away, He pleads, and spend some time in rest. He calls to those who are weary and heavy laden to come unto Him, for He is the rest that we seek. Loving, kind, gentle, patient, long suffering with my displays of flesh. There is no one else like Him. He is one of a kind. A prototype of the new creation. And we, by faith, become what He is. A new creation. All the old things have already passed away in His sight, as they should in ours.

*　　*　　*

He does not speak of my sins when I fall. He picks me up and encourages me on the journey. He doesn't tell me what I have done wrong; He instead speaks of what He has done for me. He is a friend in the truest sense of the word. He loves me with an unfailing, unconditional love.

*　　*　　*

A voice told me once that it's not about love. It's about Christ. But is not Christ God in the flesh? And God is love, is He not? And Christ manifested the very image and likeness of God by loving us to death, did He not? Therefore love is Christ and Christ is love. And the desired manifestation of God is found on the Earth when we love others as He loved us. All people; rich men, poor men, beggars and thieves. Love is not a respecter of persons. Love does not keep track of sin. It is this love that God desires of His children. A love that neither judges nor throws stones. A love that will bring us out of Religion and be the bridge that leads to Him.